Teen Suicide

Look for these and other books in the Lucent Overview series:

Abortion
Acid Rain
AIDS
Alcoholism
Animal Rights
The Beginning of Writing
Cancer
The Collapse of the Soviet Union
Dealing with Death
Death Penalty
Democracy
Drugs and Sports
Drug Trafficking
Eating Disorders
Endangered Species
Energy Alternatives
Espionage
Extraterrestrial Life
Gangs
Garbage
The Greenhouse Effect
Gun Control
Hate Groups
Hazardous Waste
The Holocaust
Homeless Children
Illiteracy
Immigration
Ocean Pollution
Oil Spills
The Olympic Games
Organ Transplants
Ozone
Population
Prisons
Rainforests
Recycling
Reunification of Germany
Smoking
Space Exploration
Special Effects in the Movies
Teen Alcoholism
Teen Pregnancy
Teen Suicide
The UFO Challenge
The United Nations
Vietnam

Teen Suicide

by Judith C. Galas

Library of Congress Cataloging-in-Publication Data

Galas, Judith C., 1946-
Teen suicide / Judith C. Galas.
p. cm. — (Lucent overview series)
Includes bibliographical references (p.) and index.
Summary: Discusses the growing problem of teenage suicide in America and offers probable causes and means of prevention.
ISBN 1-56006-148-0 (alk. paper)
1. Teenagers—United States—Suicidal behavior—Juvenile literature. 2. Suicide—United States—Prevention—Juvenile literature. 3. Suicide—United States—Juvenile literature. [1. Suicide.] I. Title. II. Series.
HV6546.G34 1994
362.2'8'0835—dc20 93-11081
CIP
AC

P.O. Box 289011, San Diego, CA 92198-9011
Printed in the U.S.A.

Contents

Introduction

MORE THAN FIVE THOUSAND young people kill themselves each year. And, suicide experts estimate, another four hundred thousand to 2 million attempt suicide each year. No one knows for sure what makes some young people want to die. No one knows for sure why the numbers of those who attempt and those who complete suicide have been increasing significantly since the 1950s.

Teen suicide puzzles some adults who think of their teen years as the best years of their lives. They wonder why the young, who should be enjoying school, dances, parties, and friends, are choosing to end their lives. They wonder why a young person would choose to die before tasting the joys of college, career, marriage, family, travel, and all life has to offer.

Many experts have tried to pinpoint the reasons for teen suicides. Psychologists and therapists, teachers and school counselors, leaders of youth groups, and researchers who study society and young people have all pointed to many things that could contribute toward the rise in teen suicide. The list of suicide culprits is long: Too much divorce, too little religion, too much television, and too little communication between parents and children have all been blamed. Absent parents, too much sexual freedom, widespread

(Opposite page) This young man, who contemplated jumping to his death, was coaxed down by friends and police. Sadly, thousands of teenagers attempt suicide every year.

use of drugs and alcohol, too many guns, not enough love, and a world that seems hostile also have been blamed for pushing young people to their deaths.

Each of these reasons has probably contributed to the suicides of many teens, but none of them, singly or together, provide the final explanation of why kids kill themselves. None of these reasons explains why some teens with problems choose to die and others with the same troubles choose to live.

Robert Litman, a psychiatrist at the Los Angeles Suicide Prevention Center, says whether a young person attempts or commits suicide is a little like a slot machine: The pull of the lever brings up pictures of plums, cherries, and bells, but no one can predict when three cherries will come up in a row and make the nickels pour out

Police restrain a young man planning to leap from the upper level of a Boston bridge. Why some teens choose to die puzzles many.

of the machine. In a similar way, no one can know for sure what series of problems or unhappy events will line up in a young person's life in such a way that death suddenly seems like the only reasonable escape. Sometimes after an attempt or a death, people can piece together what pushed the young person to suicide, but many times no one knows for sure.

The growing number of teen suicides is frightening and sad, but it is important to remember that most teenagers do not kill themselves. In 1990, the U.S. census figures showed that about 36,600,000 young people between the ages of fifteen and twenty-four lived in the United States. In that year, almost five thousand killed themselves, but 36,595,000 did not. Many of the ones who lived had the same family, social, school, or economic pressures as those who committed suicide.

The loss of those five thousand young people is tragic, not only for themselves, but also for family and friends who knew and loved them. Social workers, psychologists, parents, and friends all seek answers to why these young people died. It is only by understanding what pushes some young people to suicide that we can prevent more suicides from happening.

1
A Growing Problem

(Opposite page) *A young woman, beset by difficulties, reacts to news that she is pregnant. Faced with an often complex array of problems, today's teenagers are choosing to kill themselves in alarming numbers.*

MORE THAN THIRTY-ONE thousand people in the United States take their lives each year, according to the figures kept by the National Center for Health Statistics (NCHS). The number is large, but the number that particularly worries suicidologists, the people who study suicide, is the growing number of young people who kill themselves. The number of teen suicides has more than tripled in the past thirty years. The Centers for Disease Control reports that between 1970 and 1980 one out of every six Americans who committed suicide was a young person between the ages of fifteen and twenty-four.

In 1990, the last year the U.S. government updated its figures, 4,869 young people between the ages of fifteen and twenty-four committed suicide. Even more shocking is that various studies nationwide show that probably between four hundred thousand and eight hundred thousand young people between the ages of fifteen and twenty-four tried to kill themselves, and some estimates are as high as 2 million.

Studies in California and Kansas report that about one out of every ten teens questioned admitted to having attempted suicide. Most of those attempts were not discovered. A 1990 survey of teens listed in *Who's Who Among American High School Students* revealed that 60 percent knew a teen who had attempted or completed suicide. Even more disturbing are studies suggesting that about half of this nation's 17 million teenagers between the ages of fifteen and nineteen have thought about suicide.

According to the NCHS, a young person commits suicide about every 1 hour and 40 minutes in this country. In the 1980s, the suicide data showed a leveling off in the number of young people who committed suicide. Suicidologists hoped this leveling off would be followed by a gradual decline, but it has not. In fact, some researchers think they are starting to see a trend toward even more teen suicides and more suicides by people under the age of fifteen.

Young people between the ages of fifteen and twenty-four kill themselves at a rate of about thirteen in every one hundred thousand. This means that for every group of one hundred thousand teens, thirteen of them will die each year by their own hands. For ten- to fourteen-year-olds, the rate is one in one hundred thousand. The federal Centers for Disease Control annually logs more than two hundred suicides by ten- to fourteen-year-olds and each year sees several suicides by five- to nine-year-olds.

The third leading killer

The National Center for Health Statistics lists suicide as the third leading killer of young adults. Only accidents and murders claim more young lives. Among college students, suicide is the second leading cause of death. Many people, however, believe that if the accident numbers were reexamined, they would show suicide to be the number one killer of young adults.

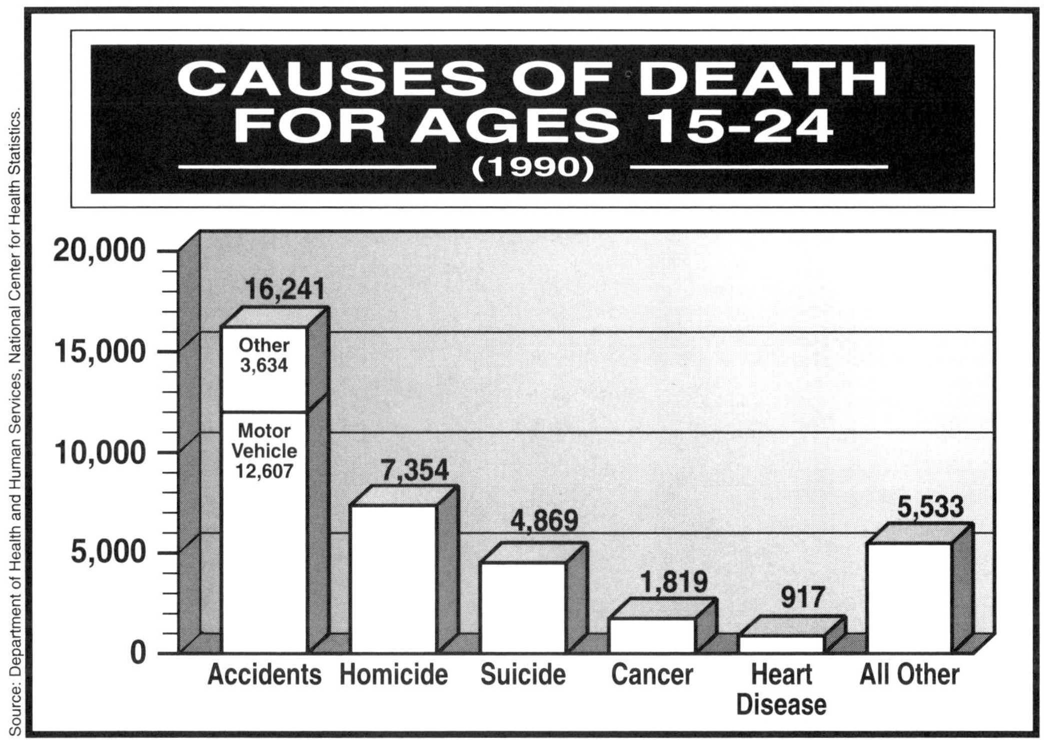

Researchers believe that many one-car accidents involving young adults may be suicides, or autocides, as some now call them. Many of these single-car accidents do not fit normal circumstances of highway accidents. Many happen when the roads are dry, visibility is good, and no other cars are on the road. Many of the young accident victims have high levels of alcohol or drugs in their bloodstreams.

Some people used to think drunkenness caused the young driver to lose control of the car. However, more and more researchers now think that a teenager who intends to commit suicide in a car first gets drunk or high to mask the fear of dying.

Other suicides are hidden within the statistics on other deaths. Some teens, for example, die from the eating disorders bulimia and anorexia. These teens may consciously or unconsciously

Many one-car accidents may actually be suicides in disguise, or "autocides." Many authorities believe that suicidal teens first get drunk or high to cover up the fear of dying.

have tried to kill themselves by damaging their bodies a little at a time. Teens who behave recklessly or who seem to be accident-prone may be flirting with suicide or may be attempting suicide.

Even with the inclusion of some teen accidents among the suicide figures, suicidologists still believe the reported number of suicides is too low. Suicide for all ages is underreported because the survivors, the authorities, and sometimes the laws make it impossible to get an accurate count.

Suicides are hidden

In some states, for example, a death certificate cannot list the cause of death as suicide unless the victim has left a suicide note. Suicidologists estimate that only about one-fifth to one-third of the people who kill themselves leave notes. In addition, in some cases the police do not find a suicide note because the relative or the friend who discovered the body has destroyed it. They might destroy it for financial reasons: Many insurance companies will not pay on life insurance policies if the insured person has committed suicide.

But often the survivors simply do not want others to know how their loved one died. Often they feel guilty. They wonder, What did we do to cause the suicide? Why did we not see the warning signs? How could we have prevented this? Sometimes they are angry at the loved one for hurting them this way. Their guilt or anger makes them avoid answering questions about the death. Because suicide often is incorrectly associated with mental illness or with severe family problems, many people also feel shame that someone they knew or loved could commit suicide. They worry about what people will think of the family.

Religious beliefs about suicide

Additionally, various religions have promoted the idea that suicide is a sin and that those who commit suicide go directly to hell for this sin. In some faiths, a suicide victim cannot be buried in cemeteries where the ground has been blessed.

Guilt, embarrassment, religious beliefs, and insurance payments do keep some people from reporting suicides, but in many cases authorities and families are just uncertain about the death. They hesitate to label the death a suicide unless they are sure.

In 1986 in Bergenfield, New Jersey, for example, Joseph Major, a high school dropout, fell two hundred feet to his death from a cliff along the Hudson River. Major had been drinking heavily on the clifftops shortly before he fell. Several of his friends thought his death was not an accident, but the authorities had no proof that Major's death was a suicide.

In October 1980, the twenty-four-year-old son

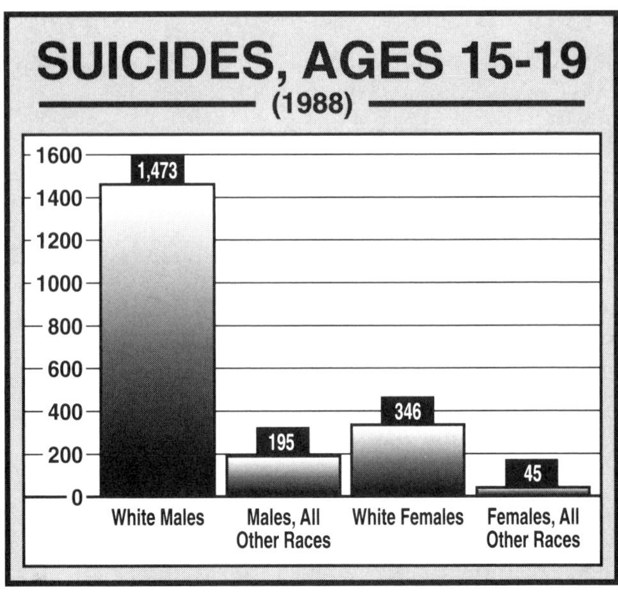

Source: Department of Health and Human Services, National Center for Health Statistics.

of actress Mary Tyler Moore died of a gunshot wound to the head. Family and friends said Richard collected guns and knew how to handle them. Officials listed his death as an accident, but suicide was considered a possibility.

Whites and blacks

Researchers and authorities cannot be certain about the number of people who really kill themselves each year, but the statistics from those who have died do give suicidologists some important information. They know, for example, that U.S. suicide victims are much more likely to be white than black. While 28,086 whites of all ages committed suicide in 1990, only 2,111 blacks committed suicide. Suicidologists think the African-American experience of having to band together to survive economic hardship and racism may give blacks a greater sense of community and membership in a group. The feeling of belonging is an important ingredient to surviving hard times and unhappiness.

Although the number of black suicides is lower than that of whites, the number of young black men who commit suicide is increasing. Some people speculate that the growing number of murders among black youth, high crime and poverty in inner-city neighborhoods, and the limited futures many young black men see for themselves may be pushing more of them to suicide.

Males and females

Suicidologists also know that males are much more likely to commit suicide than females are. The NCHS reports that in 1990, 26,461 men of all ages killed themselves, but only 6,556 females committed suicide. Of the females, only 374 black females committed suicide, the lowest number listed among white, black, and other non-white groups.

Researchers note that more females attempt

The increasing violence and crime in inner-city neighborhoods may be pushing more black youths to suicide.

suicide, but more males die from it. Cultural attitudes about violence and about dealing with emotions may help explain the differences in male and female suicide deaths and attempts.

Most cultures discourage violence in females, so females are more likely to choose less violent ways to die. They will swallow pills or make slashes across their wrists. A person using these methods may take several hours to die, so it is likely someone will come upon the victim while she is still alive.

Males, however, are more likely to hang or shoot themselves or crash their cars. Death comes more quickly from these methods, so people who use them are less likely to be rescued. Today, more and more women are using guns to end their lives, so the number of completed female suicides is expected to increase.

The different comfort levels males and females have with their emotions also play a role in keeping more females alive. In our society, males are less likely to talk about their feelings. If a

Females are more likely than males to communicate their feelings to others and thus are more likely to get help before a serious suicide attempt.

depressed man is thinking about suicide, the chances are greater that he will keep his feelings and thoughts to himself. Then one day he will take a gun and shoot himself. Females, on the other hand, talk about their feelings and what makes them sad. They are more likely to talk with a friend or counselor and will get help before they make a serious attempt on their lives.

The role of guns

Suicidologists also know other facts about suicide. The suicide rate is highest in the West—in Nevada, Montana, New Mexico, and Idaho—and lowest in the Middle Atlantic—in New York, New Jersey, and Pennsylvania. Some people think these figures reflect regional attitudes toward guns. In the West, guns are acceptable and visible, and almost every family has at least one. Many of the eastern states have stricter gun control laws. Guns are more difficult for the average person to obtain, are rarely displayed or carried, and are not routinely found in homes. More people die from gun violence in large eastern cities, but these deaths are not suicides.

More than half of the teenagers, 65 percent, who complete their suicides die of gunshot wounds. At the University of Pittsburgh, researchers reported in 1992 that of the completed teen suicides they studied, two out of three of the young victims lived in homes where adults kept guns. Those teens who attempted suicide but who did not have guns in their homes were more likely to survive their suicide attempts because they chose less lethal ways to die.

Throughout the country guns are the most common method of suicide. In New York City, however, which has tight gun-control laws, only 17 percent of the suicides result from guns. Experts conclude from the various gun and suicide studies that gun-control laws probably lower a city's suicide rate, particularly among young men.

Research reveals more

Researchers learn other things about suicide from the various studies they have done. They now know suicides are more likely to occur during the day and probably are not affected by rain, full moons, or holidays. People may feel depressed during the winter holidays if they feel alone and left out of the fun, but suicide rates do not go up in December. Instead they go up slightly in April and May. This may be because depressed people feel even sadder and more helpless when they see the spring rebirth going on everywhere around them.

Researchers' statistics also suggest that no particular religious belief seems to protect people from suicide. Years ago, people believed that those who followed Catholicism or Judaism were less likely to commit suicide because their faiths strongly denounced suicide. That assumption no longer holds true, and suicides occur among members of all faiths.

A call for help

The statistics offer a lot of facts about suicides, but they do not tell why someone wants to die. Psychologists and counselors, however, believe the majority of people who attempt suicide really do not want to die. They believe that many of those who attempt and even many of those who complete their suicides are really crying out for help. They want the unhappiness and strain in their lives to end, but they really do not want their lives to end.

An article in *Reader's Digest* helps to show that someone might commit suicide but not really want to die. An anonymous young woman wrote about the suicide of her friend, Beth. Beth had tried unsuccessfully to kill herself once before.

At a Catholic funeral, family and friends mourn the death of a young boy. Although Catholicism and Judaism both strongly denounce suicide, their followers are not less likely than other people to kill themselves.

The next time, she said, she would take cyanide, an extremely lethal poison.

The night Beth took cyanide, she did one thing before she collapsed; she asked her sorority sister to call for an ambulance. It arrived too late to save her.

A wish to live and die

Suicidologists would say Beth's suicidal thoughts were ambivalent: She wanted both to die and to live. She took cyanide, but she also asked for an ambulance. Many of those who attempt suicide are ambivalent. One teenager's suicide note shows this. He wrote, "Dear Mary, I hate your guts. Love, John." Hatred and love—the feelings flow together, and a desperate teenager can feel both at the same time.

Edwin Shneidman, a well-known suicidologist and founder of the American Association of Suicidology, rates the lethality, or deadliness, of a victim's choice of death. The lethality level is a way to measure a person's intent or wish to die. For example, if a teenager storms into her parents' bedroom while they are awake and scratches back and forth on her wrist with a letter opener until her wrist bleeds, her lethality rating would be a nonlethal *1*.

These low-lethality, easy-rescue suicides often are called parasuicides because they are similar to but not identical to a real attempt at suicide. The young woman with the scratched wrists may be in emotional trouble, but it is clear from her behavior that what she wants is her parents' attention. She wants them to know she is hurting; she does not really want to die.

If her parents ignore her or punish her for acting out, she could become suicidal and truly set upon the task of killing herself. If she waits until no one is home and shoots herself in the head

During her much-publicized marital problems with Prince Charles, rumors circulated that Princess Diana had committed parasuicide to draw attention to her emotional distress. Unlike serious suicide attempts, parasuicides are cries for help that are unlikely to result in death.

with a pistol, her attempt would have a lethality rating of 9. Her suicide attempt probably would be lethal because it is unlikely that anyone or anything could save her from this attempt.

Statistics compiled by the NCHS show that for every one hundred to two hundred teenage suicide attempts, only one is completed. This suggests that many teenagers are committing parasuicides. In contrast, one in four attempters over the age of sixty-five die. This suggests that when older people decide to take their lives they really want to die; they are not just calling out for help.

Suicide survivors have helped suicidologists better understand the thoughts and feelings of suicidal people, particularly in those days, hours, or minutes when they become firm in their decision to die. The experts cannot know for sure, however, whether those who completed their suicides really wanted to die, for even a high lethality rating cannot measure a person's feelings. Many of those who killed themselves might really have been crying out for help or attention. Many at the last moment might have regretted their decision to commit suicide. One young San Franciscan is an example of this change of mind.

Several years ago a young man attempted suicide by jumping off the Golden Gate Bridge. His

A jump off the Golden Gate Bridge is very likely to result in death. Thus, it would have a high lethality rating.

attempt would have a high lethality rating. People could assume he intended to die because few can survive such a high jump into the cold and rough Pacific Ocean. By chance, someone spotted him on the bridge, and he was rescued within minutes of hitting the water. When asked what he was thinking the moment after he jumped, he said, "I wanted to change my mind."

Understanding why

Most friends and family are not interested in whether their teenager's suicidal act had a high or low lethality rating. They want to know why their young person decided to die in the first place. Suicide specialists list several reasons teenagers attempt suicide. Some of the bigger reasons are overpowering negative thoughts, unhappy or traumatic events, and the need for revenge or attention.

All people have moments of despair, times when they feel helpless to change a bad situation or feel guilt for having done something wrong. Some suicide experts believe that when these negative feelings overpower good thoughts, the person feels too worthless and despairing to want to live. The world-famous psychiatrist Karl Menninger wrote in 1938 that these negative thoughts helped activate the aggressive feelings a person has and that this aggression played a large part in suicide. Suicide, he said, is aggression turned inward, in the same way that homicide (murder) is aggression turned outward. Menninger believed that alcoholism, drug addiction, even obesity and smoking, could be ways for people to turn on themselves and harm or eventually kill themselves.

Teenagers especially tend to turn on themselves with self-criticism. During the teen years, young people frequently measure themselves

Psychiatrist Karl Menninger described suicide as aggression turned inward.

against the accomplishments of their friends and their families' expectations for achievement. They often do not like how they look or how their social or athletic skills compare with those of other teens. Some teens deeply hate themselves. They believe they are worthless and unlovable and should not continue to live.

Sometimes an unhappy event precedes a teen's suicide. A move from an old neighborhood or a romantic breakup has been known to trigger teen suicide. Some teens kill themselves because they want to reunite with a loved one who has died. Even losses that might seem minor to one person can trigger suicidal thoughts in another.

Two teens tell why

Eugene Ellis decided to kill himself after he lost his job and broke up with his girlfriend. In a public television video called "Teenage Suicide: The Ultimate Dropout," the dark-haired teen told how he had been having trouble in school and had started roaming the streets late at night. To stop the pain he was feeling, Eugene slit his wrists, but not deeply enough to die. Days later he said he was glad he had not died: "I would have missed out on a lot of things."

Suicide as revenge

Some teenagers plan to take their lives as a way to punish people they think have been unkind, unfair, or uncaring. Absorbed with thoughts of revenge and of making others feel bad, they do not realize that when they are dead, they will not be able to see people crying over them. They will not feel any satisfaction.

In the PBS video, Carol Davis, a soft-spoken teenager, looked shy, even timid. Carol felt her

Imagining friends and family mourning over their dead body, some teenagers commit suicide as a way to punish the people in their lives who have hurt them.

schoolmates did not like her. "I was self-pitying," she says. "I wanted more attention."

In her daydreams, she said, she imagined herself dead by her own hand, and she got satisfaction from watching others cry over her body. Carol said she wanted to use her suicide as a way to get back at people: "They'll really feel bad, I thought."

Carol slashed her wrists with a knife, but not seriously enough to die. The attempt, however, scared her. With the help of a counselor she changed her focus to living rather than dying. "People would have felt bad for a while," she says, "but then they would have forgot about me. But I wouldn't have been around to enjoy anything."

Suicidal teens like Eugene and Carol struggle with the three "I"s: Life, they believe, is *in*escapable, *in*terminable, and *in*tolerable. They feel that they cannot run away from or overcome their problems. They fear that their sad feelings

Suicidal teens suffer from a persistent sadness that they fear will never go away.

Feeling powerless and unlucky, many suicidal teens are filled with a deep sense of hopelessness and despair.

will go on forever and that they will not be able to tolerate their sadness much longer. They also battle against what suicidologists describe as the three "H"s: They feel *h*elpless, *h*apless, and *h*opeless. They believe they are powerless and unlucky, and this belief fills them with despair.

Mental health experts do not know why one teenager will become overpowered by the three "I"s or the three "H"s and attempt suicide and why another teen with the same or similar experiences will weather difficulties and survive physically unharmed. In their search for information and answers about teen suicide, many people look to the teenager's family. Because the family has such a strong influence on children, many believe that a young person's decision to live or die often begins at home.

EARTHSAVER

2

Family Influence

MENTAL HEALTH EXPERTS agree that the family is the most important influence on a young person's emotional stability and growth. So when the mental health and social welfare experts try to explain the rising numbers of teen suicides, they look at the family to see if they can find the answers. No one knows for sure, however, how family life and changes in the American family affect young people and if those changes are increasing the number of teen suicides.

Recent studies

During recent decades, several noted specialists have studied the family and how it influences children and suicide. In the 1960s, Herbert Hendin, an American psychoanalyst, looked at Scandinavian families. He wanted to find out why the suicide rates in Denmark and Sweden were three times higher than in the neighboring country of Norway. While observing family life in Scandinavia, Hendin found differences in how each society raised its children.

(Opposite page) Family life is thought to be the most important influence on a young person's emotional stability and growth. To what extent changes in the American family are affecting suicide rates is an area of considerable study and debate.

In Norway, children felt their mothers' love even if they did not excel. Hendin said Norwegians had positive feelings about themselves. They were happy regardless of whether or not they were successful in their careers, and their

In the 1960s American psychoanalyst Herbert Hendin conducted a study of three Scandinavian countries. He concluded that a connection exists between family life and suicide rates.

children were allowed to express their anger.

In Sweden, however, parents placed rigid demands on their children to perform well. When Swedes failed at something, they were likely to be filled with self-hatred. In Denmark, Hendin noticed that children were raised to hold in their anger and to develop a strong dependency on their mothers.

Hendin believed held-in anger and dependency in the Danes and fear of failing in the Swedes contributed to their higher suicide rates. His work shed some light on how child-rearing practices helped to shape even adult attitudes toward dependency and self-esteem.

In the 1930s and 1940s, psychotherapist Karen Horney studied how parents' attitudes affected their children's self-esteem and feelings of security. She concluded that if the parents were indifferent or cold, or if they criticized the child for not meeting unrealistically high standards, the child would grow up feeling insecure and worthless. Today's research shows that many suicidal young people come from homes where the parents are indifferent or distant and where the lines of communication between parents and children have broken down or were never strong in the first place.

Mary's story

In her story, "I Wanted to Die," an anonymous young woman, who will be called Mary, describes the events that led to her suicide attempt when she was a high school senior. Like many suicide victims, Mary seemed successful. She was a member of the National Honor Society, editor of her school paper, and a good athlete. She was shy, however, and a little withdrawn. "I was

These Los Angeles honor students say that the pressure to succeed can often be stressful. The pressure of unrealistically high standards has pushed some teens to commit suicide.

convinced no one understood me, especially my parents," she wrote.

Her mother had died when she was small, and Mary lived with a father who was often absent because of work and a stepmother she felt did not like her. "I remember her once telling me,'I didn't have to take you, you know.'" Her stepmother made Mary feel that she was a nuisance and that caring for her was a burden.

When Mary was about fifteen, her parents started talking about divorce, and they frequently argued about her. Feeling unloved and unappreciated by her parents and believing she was the cause of their problems, Mary became obsessed with suicide.

She fell into a deep depression, gained forty pounds within a few months, and retreated to her stereo and earphones. In February of her senior year she swallowed a large number of tranquilizers and rum. She passed out on the sidewalk, and a passerby found her and called an ambulance.

Mary's parents did not want to talk about her suicide attempt. "Why did you do such a stupid thing?" was all her stepmother asked. "I'm sure she had her reasons," was all her father replied. In spite of her emotional troubles, Mary graduated number one in her class and went to a prestigious college. She was surprised to find that people liked her. Her confidence improved and she excelled in college sports. Mary not only found herself enjoying life, but she also felt appreciated and needed by her friends, her team, and her school. "I slowly began to realize that taking my own life was no longer an option," she wrote.

Parental disinterest

Mary's story is not unusual. In many families, people cannot talk to one another, or parents have a hidden hostility toward their children or a lack

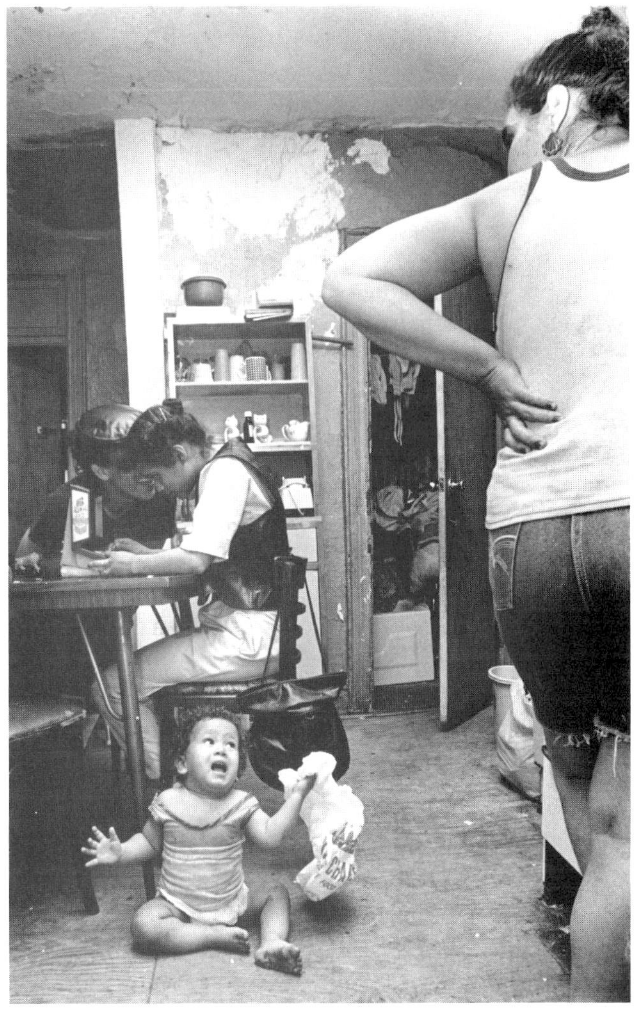

Sadly, many young people are raised in unhappy households, with parents who display little concern for their children's welfare. Often, these children grow up feeling unwanted or that they are too much trouble.

of interest in their welfare. Some studies show that one-half of the parents of suicidal teens have let their children believe they were unwanted or too much trouble.

In other homes, parents ignore their child's suicidal behaviors because they do not want to admit that the family or the child has problems. School psychologists report that when they have called a teen's home to report suicidal behaviors, they sometimes are met by defensive, even angry parents. In one case the mother said, "When my

Sexual, physical, and emotional abuse can all have the effect of destroying a young person's self-esteem.

daughter left for school, she was fine. If she's suicidal now, it must be your fault."

In some homes, parents do not take precautions to remove guns and drugs even when they know their child is suicidal. In those homes, the teenager may feel he or she simply is carrying out the family's wish that the child disappear. In many suicides, the teenager may choose to die as a way to punish hostile, rejecting, or uninvolved parents.

Abusive families

Parental disinterest hurts children emotionally, but in some homes the child is physically hurt as well. Sexual and other forms of physical abuse play a large role in destroying teenagers' self-esteem and making them feel hopeless, hapless, and helpless. Trapped between their love for and dependence on their abusive parents and their painful lives, many choose suicide as an escape.

According to Anne Cohn Donnelly of the National Committee for the Prevention of Child Abuse, 2,694,000 children were abused in 1991. Statistics from various sources confirm that about one-third of families experience some form of violence in the home, and in about one-half of those homes, children are hurt. When children are not physically touched by the violence, they fearfully witness violence between the home's adults.

Like suicide, child abuse is underreported, and many social agencies cannot handle the heavy and growing load of cases that must be investigated and prosecuted. Too often, abused children are left on their own to survive as best they can.

In his book *Kids on the Brink*, physician David B. Bergman described several teens who suffered from abuse. One teen, Jerry, from the time he was five was brutally beaten by his stepfather whenever the dad discovered even small misbehaviors.

His mentally ill mother also abused him and once came close to strangling him.

Jerry grew into a mean teenager who often intimidated female students, skipped school, and used drugs. One night Jerry swallowed and snorted a large amount of speed, a powerful and dangerous drug. Jerry went into convulsions and lost consciousness, but he was revived in the hospital emergency room. The doctors said he suffered from drug abuse and depression, both frequent side effects of abusive childhoods.

Sexual abuse

Sexual abuse also pushes many teens to suicide. A Canadian study showed that one-third of the females who had committed or attempted suicide had been sexually abused. The American statistics on sexual abuse are alarming—one in four young women are thought to be sexually molested before they reach eighteen. Most often they are molested by a male member of their family.

Sexual abuse makes a young woman feel guilty and ashamed. Minister Michael Miller, who works extensively with teen suicide issues and family problems, says sexually molested children believe they are responsible for the unwanted attention. "The children," says Miller in his book *Dare to Live*, "are always innocent, even when they don't believe they are."

Colleen's story

Dr. Bergman also wrote of Colleen, a fourteen-year-old who had been sexually molested by her father from the time she was little. Her father told her their time together was a special secret and that Mommy must never know. Colleen often was uncomfortable with her father's physical attentions, but when she reached puberty she decided that what they were doing was wrong. She be-

came angry and spilled her secret to her mother.

As too often happens in these cases, Colleen's mother did not believe her. She said Colleen must be exaggerating what happened. Surely her husband was not having sexual intercourse with his teenage daughter.

Miller estimates that 75 percent of the incest victims he has met have told him that their mothers did not believe them. Many times mothers are afraid of what will happen to them or to their families if their husbands or boyfriends are arrested for sexually abusing their daughters. Often they have known or suspected for years that the abuse was going on.

Colleen felt betrayed by both her father and her mother. Guilt, shame, and a sense of powerlessness drove her to suicide. One day when her parents went to work, she cut open both her wrists with a razor. The housekeeper found Colleen in time to save her. Colleen, the doctors said, felt abandoned by the very people she believed would love and protect her.

Like many sexually abused teens, Colleen felt great ambivalence toward her father. She hated what he was doing to her, but she loved him and did not want to hurt him or the family. Many young women like Colleen carry the guilt, shame, and anger of what has happened to them for years.

Miller recalled speaking at a church luncheon for about one hundred women. "I asked the women to bow their heads, close their eyes, and raise their hands if they had ever been sexually abused. Two-thirds of them raised their hands." When Miller asked how many of them still felt the hurt, few lowered their hands.

Young men also are sexually molested, but many therapists believe in much fewer numbers than girls. Young men are more hesitant to talk about the abuse, but just as with girls, the abuse leaves them confused and often suicidal.

Social changes affect families

Although emotional and physical abuse happens to far too many young people, many teens grow up in homes where they are not abused. Still, many experts say, today's young people live in distinctly different families than their parents or grandparents did, and stresses on today's families also are hurting young people.

Social researchers point to four significant changes during the last few decades that have made American family life more stressful: frequent family moves, an increase in families with both parents working outside the home, more single-parent families, and a high national divorce rate. Many people who work with troubled youth believe one or a combination of these changes are partly responsible for increased family stress and for the increase in teen suicide.

In the early 1900s, people rarely moved away

from the area where they were born and raised. Even in the 1940s, it was still common for young couples and their children to live near or even with their parents or older family members.

Families also had more children, so there were more older brothers and sisters looking after smaller children. Children in these large, extended families never lacked for company or supervision. Children could always find someone to talk to or someone who would make them talk if they looked like they were worried or in trouble.

Families are more mobile today and, on the average, move about eleven times in the family's lifetime. Children frequently must adjust to new schools and make new friends. Often they grow up hundreds of miles away from their extended families, and they may see their grandparents once a year or less.

Unlike today's smaller, more mobile families, many families in the early 1900s included extended family members. These large families provided children with constant company and supervision.

Some family experts believe the loss of the watchful, extended family has had a negative impact on today's children. They have no one but their often-tired parents to turn to for companionship and help.

In addition to being separated from the extended family, many children now grow up separated for the entire day from parents who have full-time jobs outside the home. In the 1960s, only about one in five mothers with children under six years old worked outside their homes. In the 1990s, that figure climbed to almost six out of every ten mothers. Shrinking wages paid to husbands and relaxed social attitudes toward women working outside the home have helped to push up the numbers of working mothers.

A significant increase in dual-income families causes many children to spend most of the day in day-care centers, separated from their parents.

Most jobs do not pay parents enough to hire live-in help to stay with their children, so most small children either go to day-care centers or to

in-home baby-sitters. Older children, however, often come home to wait for their parents. These children, often called latchkey children because of the house keys they wear around their necks, have some special problems to overcome.

After school more than three-quarters of young teens take care of themselves and often their younger siblings. Lore Nelson, a pediatrician at the University of Kansas Medical Center, thinks this is too much responsibility for young teens. Parents, she says, "expect so much responsibility out of these kids. You're expecting thirteen-year-olds to make wise decisions not only for themselves, but also for someone else."

More children are lonely

One of the biggest problems these children face is loneliness, which can lead to depression or dependence on friends who have only a child-sized amount of wisdom or experience to share. Children left alone also can make bad choices for themselves. For example, one of Nelson's teenage patients said she began drinking when she was eleven and at home without supervision.

Children raised in homes where both parents work can miss out on important adult guidance and encouragement if the parents do not take time to pay attention to their children. If the parents are busy or preoccupied with work, the children may feel they have no one who cares, no familiar confidant to turn to. They may feel that their parents do not enjoy being parents and take care of their children out of a joyless sense of duty.

Single-parent homes

In homes with only one parent, the pressure on the lone adult and children increases. Children with only one parent in the home may suffer from economic hardship and may have to fight for at-

A busy single mother enjoys a precious moment with her son. Single parents, who often suffer from exhaustion and economic hardship, are often forced to sacrifice time with their children.

tention from a parent who, all alone, must make the family's entire living and care for the children. Single parents often suffer from exhaustion and money worries.

In 1992 the Census Bureau reported that one-quarter of the nation's children younger than eighteen lived in single-parent households. In 1970, a little more than one in ten children lived with one parent. Now half of the children born in 1980 will spend some of their childhoods in a single-parent home.

Unmarried mothers

Many single-parent homes are headed by unmarried mothers. One-fourth of all the babies born in 1992 were born to unmarried mothers. Studies show these women are poorer, less educated, and more dependent on welfare than those who were married at the time the child was born. Their children probably will have slightly harder lives than children born into families with two parents or with one parent where the mother had been married or is better educated.

In Bellevue Hospital in New York City, two-thirds of the teens the hospital sees for attempted suicide come from one-parent homes. Most of these young people come from areas of New York City where poverty, violence, and drugs are all too common.

Many family and child experts point to the increase in single-parent households as one of the reasons teen suicides are increasing. But other experts are quick to defend the single-parent family. They say there is little evidence to show that simply being raised in a single-parent home damages children or drives them to suicide. They admit that these children are more likely to have behavioral or school problems. But, these experts say, most of their problems come from the poverty that often follows single parenthood or from the family upsets that led up to the parents' divorce

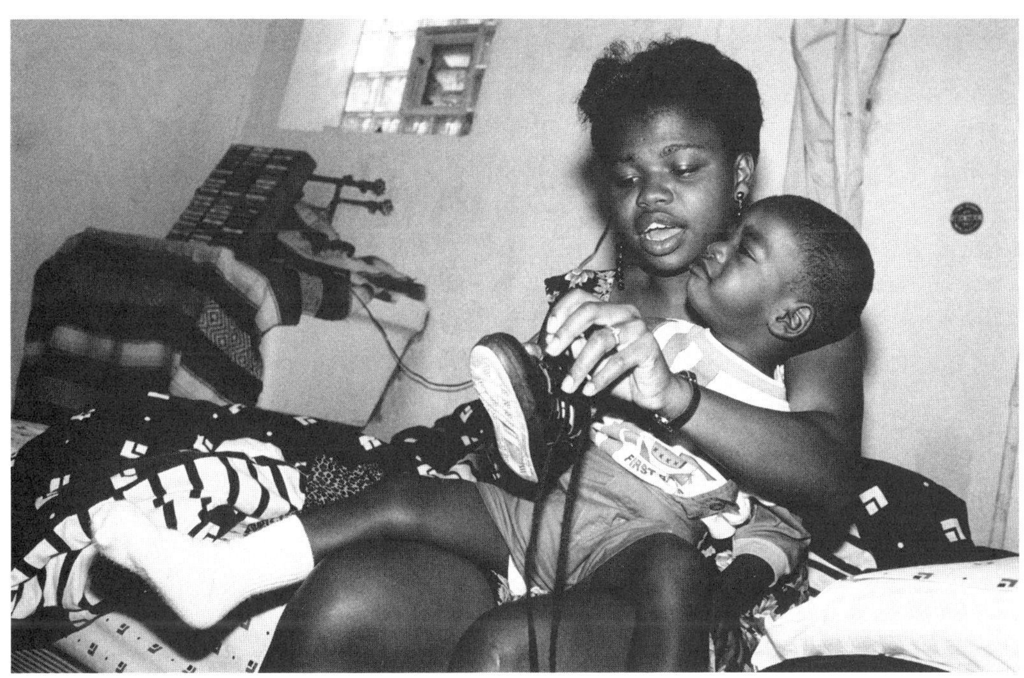

A nineteen-year-old single parent prepares her son for day care. Raised in a drug-infested, crime-ridden housing project, this young mother is struggling to provide a better life for her son by going to college.

or separation. The problems are not caused by parental unconcern or neglect.

Frank F. Furstenburg Jr., a sociologist at the University of Pennsylvania, points to a long-term study comparing children in divorced, one-parent families with children in two-parent families. The study, he says, shows that differences in the children's mental health or problems with school or the police are small and that even many of those problems resulted from the divorce.

Divorce affects suicide

Experts cannot agree on whether teenage suicide is up because families move too frequently, or because both parents work, or because children have only one parent. Many, however, believe there is a direct relationship between the rising rate of divorce and the rising rate of teen suicide.

Dr. Mary Giffin, a specialist in the field of teen suicide, points out that Americans have the high-

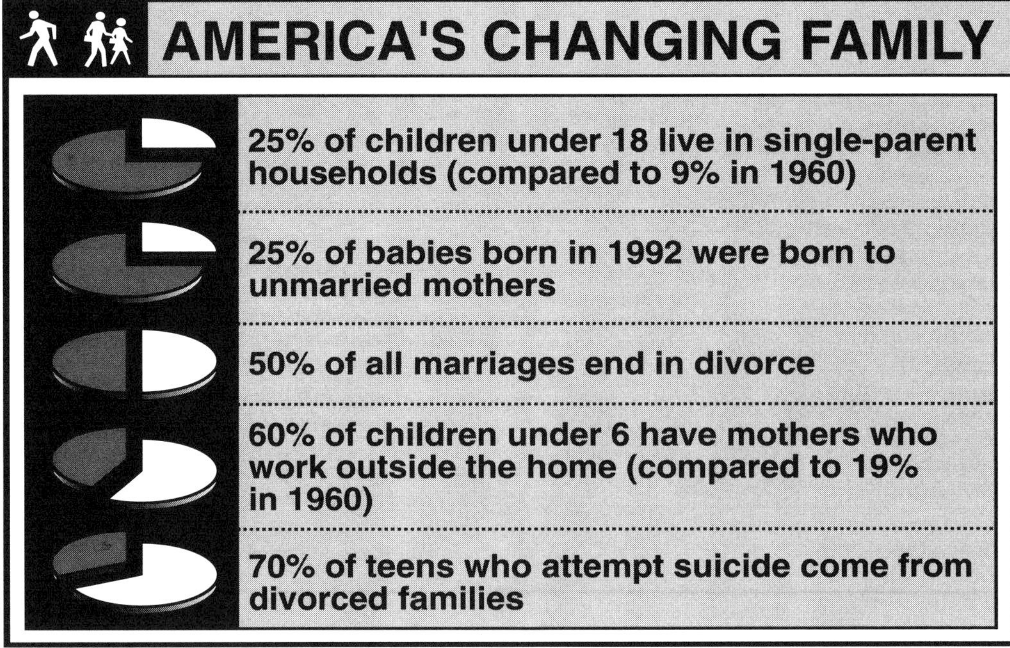

est divorce rate in the world and that both the divorce rate and the teen suicide rate have tripled in the last twenty years. One in every two American marriages ends in divorce, so it is not surprising that only about one-third of teens live with both birth parents. What shocks many therapists and suicidologists is that seven out of the ten teenagers who attempt suicide come from divorced families.

Some people who study trends in family life believe that today's career-focused adults are selfish and more concerned about their individual lives and careers than the welfare of their children and the family. This selfishness and lack of love, they believe, increases both the divorce rate and the teen suicide rate.

Divorce does not affect suicide

Other family experts, however, reject the idea that too much selfishness and too little love are behind the high divorce and teen suicide rates. Today, couples live longer than couples of the early 1900s, say these family experts. In the 1900s, the average marriage lasted twelve years before one of the spouses died. Because modern couples live longer, they have more opportunity to grow apart. Today's couples do not divorce more often because they are less concerned about their children than couples of earlier times. They choose to divorce rather than to live forty, fifty, or sixty years in an unhappy marriage.

Many therapists also are quick to point out that it is not the divorce itself that causes children problems, but rather the pressures that brought on the divorce and the anger that exploded during the divorce. These emotional tensions may be what is pushing teenagers to think of suicide. Financial worries after the divorce may also bring stress for the single parent and the children.

Some teenagers, therapists say, find it more difficult to handle conflicts in their lives when a big conflict like divorce is draining their emotional energy. School or social problems that would seem minor to a young person from a happy home may feel major to a teen already struggling with fighting parents.

Divorce rates and suicide rates may be traveling higher together, but no one can be certain that one is causing the other. What is certain is that families and children both seem beset with problems.

Suicide by example

If the family clearly plays any role in teen suicide, it is in the example it sets of how people should face and deal with problems. Studies indicate that a tendency toward suicide probably is not inherited, but young people can learn by example from parents, relatives, and even older siblings that suicide is an acceptable way out of life's problems. In her book *Suicide: The Hidden Epidemic,* Margaret Hyde says that experience suggests "that a person close to someone who commits suicide may always carry the idea that in some way death is a way out of extremely stressful circumstances."

Families blamed for suicides

Whether through example, indifference, abuse, economics, or divorce, being single mothers or absent fathers, working too much or listening too little, parents frequently hear the media or family experts say they are responsible for the rise in teenage suicide. In fairness to the American family, many people argue against the idea that children experienced happier, simpler, and more loving families in years past. They do not accept the idea that children are killing themselves in

An exhausted teenage mother collapses in a chair with her son after a long day's work. While many people blame today's parents for the rise in teenage suicide, others blame society.

greater numbers today because the American family suddenly has more problems.

Sociologist Stephanie Coontz, who wrote *The Way We Never Were: American Families and the Nostalgia Trap*, says the idea of happier families is pure myth. In every period in history, she points out, families have experienced child abuse and incest, sexism and racism, alcoholism and drug addiction, teen pregnancy and grinding poverty. These problems, which have existed in families throughout history, did not increase the teen suicide rate in other centuries.

The increase in teen suicide, some believe, comes not so much from what is happening inside the family as from what is happening in the society that surrounds the family. Young people may be killing themselves in greater numbers because the world, not their families, has turned more frightening, less predictable, and more stressful.

3

Social Pressures

(Opposite page) An anarchist youth, often labelled a social rebel, watches passersby from a doorway in New York City. Some people believe that suicides have increased because society has lost control of its citizens.

THE SOCIETY A young person lives in has a strong impact on how he or she feels about life and the future. Many sociologists and psychologists have tried to understand and explain why some people attempt suicide. The French sociologist Emile Durkheim is credited with developing the first ideas about the relationship between society and suicide. In his famous book *Suicide*, published in 1897, Durkheim asserted that suicides happened when society broke down and lost its influence over its citizens. Suicides, he said, did not happen in societies where people felt connected to each other and to their social institutions.

Durkheim believed that the amount of control a society had over its citizens caused suicides to increase or decrease. The more control a society had, the fewer the suicides. For example, Durkheim credited religion and church rules with reducing suicides. Although a nonbeliever, Durkheim believed religious institutions made people feel connected to a group larger than themselves. These connections reduced the likelihood of suicide.

Many theories have been developed since Durkheim first tried to describe the types of suicides and what caused them. But Durkheim's de-

French sociologist Emile Durkheim has been credited with developing the first ideas about the relationship between society and suicide.

scription of two types of suicide—egoistic and anomic—remain helpful in trying to understand why some young people attempt suicide.

An egoistic suicide is caused by a person's sense of self as being isolated and apart from others. These suicides occur when a person's ties to society are too weak or too few. For example, a teen who does not feel a part of a social group, who does not belong to any clubs, or who is new in the neighborhood or school may suffer from a lack of social connection. This young person may be susceptible to egoistic thoughts of aloneness and isolation.

An anomic suicide is caused by a person's feeling detached or alienated from his or her world because some crisis shatters the person's social or family ties. A young person, for example, may lose his or her sense of connection through a death in the family, a broken romance, a lost job, or a move that means making new friends in a new school. In young people, anomie, or a feeling of deadness and emptiness, also can develop when teens feel threatened by society and its pressures. They may attempt suicide as a way to break their connections and avoid these pressures.

An athlete attempts suicide

Durkheim might have described athlete Kathy Love Ormsby's attempt in 1986 as an anomic suicide resulting from pressures she tried to escape. In Indianapolis, at the track championships for the National Collegiate Athletic Association, the twenty-one-year-old track star tried to kill herself by running off a bridge. A few days before, Ormsby had set the U.S. women's collegiate record for 10,000 meters. But in Indianapolis she was having a hard time getting the lead in the championships. *Sports Illustrated* reported that just after she had moved up to fourth in the pack of runners, she left the track and ran straight out of the arena without breaking stride.

Ormsby apparently crossed a baseball diamond, climbed over a seven-foot fence, and ran down a main street toward the bridge crossing the White River. From there she ran off the bridge and fell seventy-five feet. Ormsby survived the fall but was paralyzed from the waist down. The accident was listed as an attempted suicide.

Everyone who knew her was shocked. Ormsby had been the valedictorian of her high school class and had graduated with a 99-plus average. She had been so admired by her peers and teachers that her high school held a day in her honor. She was the only athlete in the school's history to have her jersey retired. At North Carolina State she was a star runner. Her physics professor described her as "a model student-athlete."

Pressure to succeed

Ormsby's father told the local newspaper that he thought the tremendous pressure put on young people today to succeed had pushed his daughter to suicide. Her high school coach thought Ormsby put a great deal of pressure on herself. "If she didn't come in first she had a tendency to think that she was letting other people down. Winning was not just for herself," he said. He thought her decision to die had been building for some time.

After she had broken the 10,000-meter record, Ormsby had told a reporter that she was trying to learn to do her best for herself and for God. Did she decide to die because she could not take the embarrassment of coming in fourth or third? Did she feel as if a less than perfect record would shame her parents, her school, or her God? Did the daily stress to succeed and compete finally

Pressure to succeed may have influenced track star Kathy Love Ormsby to attempt suicide by running off a bridge.

wear her down? No one but Kathy Ormsby knows for sure, but similarities to her story can be found in the lives of other young people who choose to die rather than face being less than perfect.

Japan, for instance, has a high teen suicide rate. In her book *Too Young to Die*, Francine Klagsbrun noted that twice as many Japanese young people between the ages of fifteen and twenty-four commit suicide than do teens in the United States. She believes the intense social pressure to succeed contributes to the large number of teen suicides.

During the time of the school year called "Examination Hell," Japanese teens take the exams that will set their futures. The results of the exams determine which universities will accept them, which companies will hire them, and which careers and incomes they will have for the rest of their lives. The pressure to do well in school is tremendous on Japanese children of all ages.

In Japan, where students feel tremendous social pressure to succeed, the teen suicide rate is among the highest in the world.

Even four-year-olds worry about which grade school will accept them. It is not surprising that Japan has one of the world's highest teenage suicide rates.

In addition to pressures to do well and to succeed, young people are surrounded by social stresses. Many of the people studying teenage suicide think three areas in our society may influence young people vulnerable to consideration of suicide: the entertainment industry and its depiction of violence, the pressures that come with greater sexual freedom, and the fears that result from knowing about wars and civil unrest worldwide.

The role of television

Since he or she was small, the average American teenager has watched one thousand hours of television a year, or about three hours a day. In contrast to that, the average teenager with two working parents spends about fourteen minutes a day talking to his or her parents. Television isolates family members from one another by reducing the amount of time people communicate. Stereo headphones and video games reduce the amount of interaction people have with each other even further.

In addition to the isolation it creates, television also creates a casual attitude toward violence and death. Those who study suicide trends believe television creates a social environment in which violence and death become ordinary and acceptable. In her book *Dead Serious*, Jane Leder reports that the average child will see twenty thousand killings on television before high school graduation. These deaths desensitize children to the finality of death and to the emotional pain that comes with losing a loved one.

Actors die only to come alive again in another

The average American watches three hours of television a day. Some believe that the violence, isolation, and lack of problem-solving skills associated with television contribute to the high suicide rate among young people.

movie. Most of those who die on television do not seem to feel much pain; their deaths are quick and frequently bloodless. Television movies do not have much time to spend on how the person suffered before he or she died or how the death affected the victim's family.

Some believe television's half-hour programs give children the impression that life comes in clean, easily solved segments. The young hero or heroine on a 30-minute program gets in and out of trouble in 22.5 minutes—the length of the show after commercials. Some psychologists believe young people grow up with the idea that problems should be solved quickly. When their problems go on for days, they wonder why their life is so much harder than anyone else's.

Television also is criticized for encouraging young people to passively observe other people's lives rather than be actively involved in their own. Television does not require the viewers to problem solve. They do not have to develop skills in communication, in working out differences with others, or in trying to understand someone else's point of view. All a viewer has to do is sit and watch.

Those who study teen suicide believe the violence, isolation, and lack of problem-solving skills associated with television make young people more vulnerable to suicide. Their real-life problems seem too impossible compared to those on television, and death seems too easy and painless.

The music industry

Many people believe the music industry also encourages young people to see suicide as desirable. In October 1984, a nineteen-year-old shot himself in the head after listening to Ozzy Os-

bourne's song "Suicide Solution" for several hours. The boy's father sued Osbourne, claiming the lyrics encouraged his son to die. The attorney representing the father said he had received at least twenty calls from parents testifying that their children killed themselves after listening to Osbourne.

Other music groups also have been accused of inciting suicide. The British heavy metal rock group Judas Priest was said to have inspired a teen suicide pact. Another group, Metallica, was criticized for its song "Fade to Black," which advises that death would be better than living in this world. Two teenage girls left a suicide note containing Metallica lyrics on the windshield of a car.

The music of heavy metal rock group Judas Priest was blamed for inspiring a teen suicide pact.

The lawsuits against Osbourne were dismissed on constitutional grounds of free speech. The courts have never convicted any music group of inciting suicides. Many parents and educators, however, feel that lyrics encouraging suicide send the message to troubled teens that suicide is an acceptable solution to their problems.

Sexual freedom

People who work with teenagers also believe that sex has become an emotional and physical threat to young people. Many teens become sexually active while they still think through their problems as children do. Inexperienced in sex and love, they find the pain of losing someone they have been sexually intimate with more than they can bear. Some young people believe adults will not take their relationship problems seriously, and they feel alone and isolated with their problems.

Statistics show that sexual activity among young people is increasing, and with this escalation has come increased danger. In a news feature

A pregnant fifteen-year-old discusses prenatal care with a medical worker. The fear of revealing a pregnancy to their parents has driven some young women to suicide.

on the pressures facing teens, the *Kansas City Star* reported a survey showing that in 1990 just over half of the fifteen- to nineteen-year-old young women surveyed said they had sex. Twenty years ago just under one-third of women in this age group said they had sex.

Besides the increase in sexual activity, this same survey reported that most teenage sex is unprotected because most young people do not use condoms. Cases of gonorrhea have increased dramatically, and hepatitis B and AIDS are real dangers. A total of more than nine thousand AIDS cases have been reported nationally among thirteen- to twenty-four-year-olds. Faced with the fear and shame of catching or having a dreaded disease, some teens take their lives.

Fear of pregnancy

Those who work with suicidal youth know that fear of pregnancy has also pushed young girls to suicide. The pregnancy rate for fifteen- to nineteen-year-old Americans is double the rate in any other industrialized nation. More than 1 million girls become pregnant each year in the United States, and four out of five are unmarried.

Many young women are afraid to tell their parents they are pregnant. They fear they will be rejected or forced out of the family home. Their shame and fears keep them from seeing a doctor about their pregnancy and from seeing a counselor about their fears. Parents have reported sad stories of losing their daughters to suicide because the young women were too frightened to admit they were pregnant.

Gay teens

Homosexual teenagers also are troubled by sex. Instead of fearing pregnancy, they fear people finding out they are gay or lesbian. David La-Fontaine, the lobbying director for the Coalition for Lesbian and Gay Civil Rights, estimates that about one-third of the estimated 1 million teen suicide attempts are committed by gay youth. "They are trapped in an environment that is overwhelmingly hostile," he said in an interview with *New York Native*.

The *Advocate*, a gay newspaper, reports that each year an estimated fifteen hundred gay youth kill themselves because they cannot continue to live in a world that hates gays. Gay youth are particularly vulnerable to suicide because negative attitudes and hostility toward gays in America keep them from talking to others about their lives and their problems. Poor self-esteem, depression, and isolation, all too common in suicidal people, particularly affect gay youth because their lives are often more difficult than for other teenagers. More than 90 percent of gay men and lesbians report they have been verbally or sexually assaulted because they are gay. Many are rejected by their families.

A staff member of Covenant House, a shelter for homeless youth, told the story of Michael, who at fifteen was kicked out of his home when

Students from a high school in New York City for lesbian and gay youths. Negative attitudes and hostility toward gays in America make gay youths particularly vulnerable to suicide.

his stepfather and mother found out he was gay. Michael ended up on the streets of New York, where he became a drug addict and a prostitute. He found help at Covenant House, but his road to recovery and self-esteem was not easy.

The day he was to leave Covenant House, a recovering drug addict and a twenty-year-old man with a future, Michael attempted suicide. He slit his wrists because he feared going out in the world on his own. He feared that as a recovering addict and a homosexual, he would not be strong enough to succeed on his own. He would let down all the friends at Covenant House who believed in him.

The world seems hostile

In addition to problems brought on by television and by greater sexual freedom, the world itself grows more confusing and hostile. Homicides have increased among teenagers. All the major newspapers have carried stories about the large numbers of students who now carry guns to school and about the schools that have hired full-time police to search students for weapons.

A sign warns high school students that they must submit to a metal detector scan before entering the school building. The prevalence of weapons in schools causes many young people to live in constant fear.

Thousands of teens are homeless. They may have been abandoned by their families, fallen through the social service cracks, or run away from difficult situations. These young people become victims of the violence of prostitution rings, drug dealers, and street crimes. Studies of homeless and runaway youth show a large number of these teens are depressed and suicidal.

Other studies show that even among teens who have relatively comfortable lives, the ongoing troubles in the world make them feel confused and uneasy. Nightly newscasts of war crimes in places such as Bosnia and South Africa, widespread famine in Somalia, and civil unrest in the Mideast, Central America, or even Los Angeles give young people the feeling that their world is unsafe and unstable.

"When I was growing up, you didn't worry about getting shot at school. You didn't worry about getting AIDS," says Daryl Lynch, a doctor who specializes in adolescent medicine. "You think these [kids] are in their golden years and they should be out playing. It's just not there for them."

Growing uncertainty

In American society continuing racial unrest and confusion over the changing roles of men and women also create feelings of disappointment and uncertainty. The United States traditionally has prided itself on being a land of equal opportunity for all. News about the Los Angeles riots, reports about the huge number of black families living in poverty, and stories of violence by police against racial minorities make many teens perceive this country as hypocritical and unfair.

Homeless teens spending the night in a park. A large number of homeless and runaway youths are depressed and suicidal.

The violence and racial unrest in American society became manifest during the Los Angeles riots. Confronted daily with disturbing images such as this, many teens express little hope for a better future.

Today's young people also are growing up during a time of uncertainty about how men and women should treat each other. Young women are told they can have everything—career, marriage, and children. But they see the women in their lives struggling to juggle these many pressures. Many women choose to drop out of the competition for schools and jobs rather than face the burden of having it all. Some, like Kathy Ormsby, think suicide will make the choices for them.

Young men are told that men and women should be treated equally, but many wonder if the pressure to get a good job and buy an expensive house and car does not rest more heavily on men. Many are confused about what young women expect from them.

The world, with its wars and racial and ethnic unrest, feels unsafe. Changing social attitudes toward women and men make life seem uncertain. These fears and uncertainties add to the pressures in a young person's life, and make some at-risk teens look to suicide as a way to ease these pressures.

Stress affects teens

Adolescent admissions to psychiatric hospitals increased 35 percent between 1975 and 1986. Some of those increased admissions resulted from more public acceptance of mental illness and mental health care. Hospital marketing programs also have convinced more parents that their children need help. Some of the increased admissions, however, resulted from the same social and family stresses that are believed to be contributing to teen suicide.

Boston psychologist David Elkind thinks today's youth are not being protected from stress and problems as they were years ago. Elkind, who was quoted in the April 1991 issue of *American Legion* magazine, said, "As a nation we've stopped doing that. Kids have more freedom today to engage in premarital sex and to experiment with drugs and alcohol." These new freedoms, coupled with high divorce rates and family stresses, put extreme pressures on young people. "They may not be ready to handle the demands that are placed on them," Elkind said.

The pressure to engage in premarital sex is a stress that may contribute to teen suicide.

Some young people respond to stress and problems in their lives by falling into depression. Others respond by using drugs and alcohol. Among all the uncertainties surrounding suicide, two areas remain quite clear. Depression frequently leads to suicide, and young people who abuse drugs and alcohol markedly increase their chances of becoming suicidal and of dying.

4

Drugs, Alcohol, and Depression

DRUG AND ALCOHOL abuse appears so frequently in young people who have attempted suicide that suicidologists list substance abuse as one of the major warning signs for a possible suicide attempt. Several studies since the 1980s have shown that a high percentage of suicide victims was addicted to drugs or alcohol. Psychiatrist David Brent at Pittsburgh's Western Psychiatric Institute and Clinic, for example, found that one-third of the sixty-seven suicidal teenagers he studied were drug or alcohol abusers. Another study in Louisville, Kentucky, found that 70 percent of the teens studied were abusers.

People who abuse drugs and alcohol and those who attempt suicide have much in common. Both groups are likely to be depressed, feel hopeless, and have a negative attitude about life and themselves. Brent's study, for example, found that of the sixty-seven teens he studied, 40 percent also were depressed. For some people, drugs and alcohol cause the depression that leads to suicide. For others, ongoing depression makes them turn to drugs and alcohol as an escape from sadness. Regardless of whether the substance abuse or the

(Opposite page) A depressed and suicidal young woman who suffers from drug and alcohol addiction struggles to come to terms with her self-destructive life-style. A high percentage of suicidal teens is addicted to drugs or alcohol.

depression comes first, depression or drug abuse almost always leads a young person to thoughts of suicide or suicide attempts.

Persistent sadness

Depression is an often temporary form of mental illness that makes a person feel deeply and inescapably sad. Some studies show that among teenage suicides, 40 percent suffered from major depression. Other studies suggest that more than half of the people who have committed suicide suffered from depression before they killed themselves.

Everyone feels unhappy now and then, and many even say they are depressed. But a truly depressed person feels deep unhappiness all the time. Because adults have had more experience riding out life's ups and downs, they tend to weather depression a little better than younger people, who are less experienced in dealing with their emotions. Teenagers focus on how they feel at the moment and frequently believe their sadness will last forever. They may believe that life will never get better than it is right now. Adults who feel depressed can recall happier moments in their lives. These recollections help them put the sad feelings they have in perspective. Teenagers may not have as many memories to fall back on. Their lives are too short to offer them much perspective.

Teenagers also are more likely than adults to see even moderate problems as being major and to interpret small misunderstandings or personal slights in the most negative light. Depressed teenagers frequently are touchy and withdrawn and are often difficult to associate with. The natural changes in the hormones that affect a young person's changing body and moods cause some of these emotional swings. Sometimes inexperi-

Teenagers who suffer from severe depression often are withdrawn and have difficulty getting along with others.

ence in communicating or in knowing how to interpret what others are saying and doing makes a young person feel emotional.

Depression in children

Until recently, many experts in the mental health professions did not think depression existed before adolescence. More and more therapists now report depression even in children as young as three. Studies show a direct relationship between emotional losses and depression in young children. Infants, for example, have become depressed after being separated from their mothers. They become withdrawn and fearful and sometimes lie passively in their cribs without crying.

Children sometimes behave differently than adults when they are depressed. Depressed adults

Even young children can suffer from depression. Unlike depressed adults who tend to become lethargic and sleepy, depressed children often become aggressive and hyperactive.

often become lethargic and sleepy, but depressed children may become aggressive or overly active to the point of being out of control. Their activity prevents people from seeing them as depressed.

Because many young people live on the fine line between childhood and young adulthood, many experts in child and adolescent psychology suggest these warning signs as clues to whether a young person is depressed:

- persistent sadness
- low self-concept
- aggressive or overly active behavior
- tendency to become easily and greatly disappointed
- physical complaints such as headaches and stomachaches
- sleep problems or overwhelming fatigue

Young people who display three or more of these warning signs should see a school counselor, social worker, or therapist. Teens who notice these signs in their friends should tell their school counselor.

Teenage depression

Lots of teenagers get depressed. In one survey, every teenager said he or she had been depressed at one time. These same teenagers, however, believed that only about one in ten of their friends had ever been depressed. These answers suggest that depressed teens see their sadness as something they alone feel, so their depression makes them feel different from others.

Another study showed that among teenagers depression came in second only to the common cold in its frequency. Unlike the common cold, however, depression can be fatal. Thoughts of suicide frequently enter the minds of people who feel helpless, hapless, and hopeless—the three feelings strongly associated with depression.

What also worries many therapists who deal with depressed and suicidal people is that frequently these patients are still in danger of committing suicide after they come out of their depressions. Therapists warn families that the end of depression does not necessarily mean their young person is safe from suicide. Many family members and friends are so relieved to see the depressed teen smiling again that they do not want to believe the young person still is suicidal, and they do not continue to watch for warning signs of suicide.

Depression is characterized by a lack of energy and the inability to make decisions. So a troubled teen who is depressed may not have the energy to carry out a suicide plan. When the depression lifts, the teen suddenly may have the ability to plan his or her death, to make decisions about how and when it will happen, and to carry out those plans.

What makes a person depressed? Mental health experts say there are two main types of depression: emotional and clinical.

Emotional depression

Emotional depression is situational; that is, it relates to a particular situation, to something occurring in people's lives to make them feel sad or stressed. Everyone feels some stress every day. In fact, even good things can bring on stress. Buying a house or car, getting married, having a baby, starting a new job, or even buying a dog can all cause stress.

People suffering from depression, however, have experienced more negative stresses: a death, a divorce, unemployment, a move, an injury, or an illness. Breaking up with a boyfriend or girl-

Experiencing a death, a move, or divorce can trigger severe depression in teens.

Brothers comfort each other at their mother's grave. While the death of a parent is indeed traumatic for a child, studies indicate that it may not be as emotionally scarring as previously thought.

friend, not making a team, or not getting accepted into a particular school could trigger stress and depression in teens. Interviews with depressed people who attempted suicide show they experienced four times the usual number of negative stresses in the months preceding their suicide attempt.

Researchers once thought the death of a parent, particularly of the mother, would put a child into a dangerous depression. Recent studies, however, seem to indicate that a parent's death might not be a child's most life-altering emotional tragedy. Children certainly become depressed when a parent dies, but research from the University of Michigan suggests that this depression may not have as lasting an effect as other childhood hurts.

Childhood trauma

Michigan sociology professor William J. Magee has studied the connections between depression and childhood trauma. "It seems," he says, "that if you can escape [a parent's death] intact when you're a teenager, you're home free." Other traumas, however, may have a more lasting impact.

Magee and other researchers at the university studied adults who suffered from depression. They found that the highest rate of adult depression was among people whose childhood had included divorce, violence, mental illness, or alcoholism. Their study, released in 1993, suggests that children who survive these traumas without obvious signs of deep depression or suicide attempts may experience these emotional setbacks later in life. Because these traumas continue in a child's life over a long period of time, they may have more opportunity to damage a young person's sense of security and self-esteem. This damage may surface during the adult years.

Clinical depression

Some mental health specialists believe more and more people are experiencing more negative stresses. They have referred to these modern times as the Age of Depression, both for youth and adults worldwide. Some researchers wonder if widespread and growing environmental pollution may be affecting people's biological chemistry. Perhaps, they say, changes in the environment could be responsible for some of the depression that results from chemical imbalances in the body or chemical attacks on the body and its nervous system.

No one has proved any definite links between depression and changes in body chemistry due to pollution. But mental health experts are quite familiar with depression caused by chemical imbalances in the body or tendencies toward depression that might be inherited. This form of depression is called clinical or chronic depression. Clinical depression lasts longer than emotional or situational depression. Some forms of clinical depression can last a lifetime, but most can be controlled with drugs.

Serotonin affects the brain

Researchers are studying the relationship between body chemistry and suicides. In fact, some researchers are beginning to think there are biological differences between people who attempt suicide as a cry for help and those who truly intend to kill themselves. One of these differences

Some researchers speculate that environmental pollution could be responsible for some of the depression that results from chemical imbalances in the body.

may be lower levels of the brain chemical serotonin in people who complete their suicides.

Alec Roy of Albert Einstein College of Medicine reported a study showing that male prisoners who had attempted suicide had lower levels of serotonin than prisoners who had never attempted it. In Pittsburgh, researcher Victoria Arango compared the brains of twenty suicide victims with the brains of those of the same sex and age who died from other causes. The brains of the twenty who died from suicide showed signs of having reduced levels of serotonin. Researchers are just beginning to understand the connections between suicide and serotonin. They are not certain exactly how serotonin affects the brain or how to adjust serotonin levels to reduce a person's tendency toward suicide.

Social researchers have been frustrated by their inability to come up with definite theories on how society and families help to cause or to prevent suicides. The answers to questions about suicide, some scientists believe, may come instead from biology, from studying the human brain and the chemicals that affect a person's mood and aggression. These biological conditions in children could be inherited from their parents. Although many experts remind people that suicide is not genetically passed down, the tendency to commit suicide because of chemical imbalances might be.

Mental illness

Some forms of mental illness, researchers have found, may also be a trait among some people who attempt suicide. Some teens are diagnosed with mental illnesses such as manic-depression or schizophrenia. Manic-depressives suffer from dramatic mood swings that take them from feeling excessively and unreasonably happy and active to feeling extremely sad, depressed, or hostile. This form of mental illness can be controlled with medication.

Some teens suffer from schizophrenia, a mental illness that forces them to withdraw and to live in unreal and frightening worlds. Schizophrenics hear voices or see people others cannot hear or see. These voices and people terrify them. This disease can be tempered with medication.

Ironically, manic-depressives and schizophrenics are more likely to consider suicide when their medications have made their lives feel more normal than when they are suffering from their disease. It is when they are thinking clearly that they look at the future as a lifetime of falling in and

A painting by a young schizophrenic woman illustrates her intense fear and isolation. Teens who suffer from mental illness often have a distorted sense of reality.

out of delusions and mood swings and decide they do not want to continue to struggle with their mental illnesses.

Although some people who commit suicide have been diagnosed with a true mental illness, the majority of people who become depressed or suicidal are not mentally ill. Most people who attempt suicide have been overwhelmed by a temporary problem that they believe they cannot escape or solve. All too often, drugs and alcohol play a large role in clouding their judgment and in making them depressed and suicidal. Study after study has found a direct link between teen suicide attempts and alcohol.

Alcohol and drug abuse

According to the 1991 College Alcohol Survey, one in four deaths of college students are associated with alcohol. These students either commit suicide while under the influence of alcohol or are involved in accidents because alcohol affects their judgment or ability to behave in a safe manner.

Young people can fall into a dangerous drinking cycle. They drink to have fun and to be social, but their drinking causes problems: They may miss school or do poorly in their classes or at their part-time jobs. They may fight more with friends and family members so their personal relationships become unpleasant. All these negatives make them depressed, which then makes them drink to feel better about themselves. This cycle can deeply affect how young people see themselves and can make them feel inadequate, stupid, unsuccessful, and fearful of their futures. Without counseling, these young people may try to solve problems of low self-esteem and depression by dying.

The strong relationship between suicide and the

use of alcohol and drugs makes these substances particularly dangerous for teenagers. Brain depressants, such as barbiturates, anti-anxiety drugs, and alcohol, and brain stimulants, such as amphetamines, cocaine, and weight-reducing drugs, impair judgment, make people more impulsive, and produce severe mood disturbances. These include temporary and intense suicidal depressions. Hallucinogens like PCP or LSD actually set up murderous behaviors.

Drug overdoses common

Drugs not only alter people's moods and behaviors, they also provide one of the most common ways for young people to commit suicide. Of the five hundred teens and children seen in one pediatric emergency room, 88 percent had tried to kill themselves by swallowing a drug overdose. Over-the-counter and prescription

Although many young people begin using alcohol for social reasons, some teens fall into a dangerous drinking cycle that causes them many problems.

drugs are easy to get; most can be found in the young person's own home.

Study after study also proves that drugs or alcohol helps a teenager make the decision to die. Large numbers of suicidal young men and women had been drinking or had taken drugs immediately before their attempts. They did not take these substances to kill themselves but to reduce the anxiety and natural self-restraint they should have had about dying.

Suicide indicators

Drug and alcohol abuse also seems to be an indicator of which youths are likely to attempt suicide. Karl Menninger, who founded the internationally famous Menninger Clinic in 1920 in Topeka, Kansas, over the years saw both substance abuse and suicide as addictive and deadly behaviors.

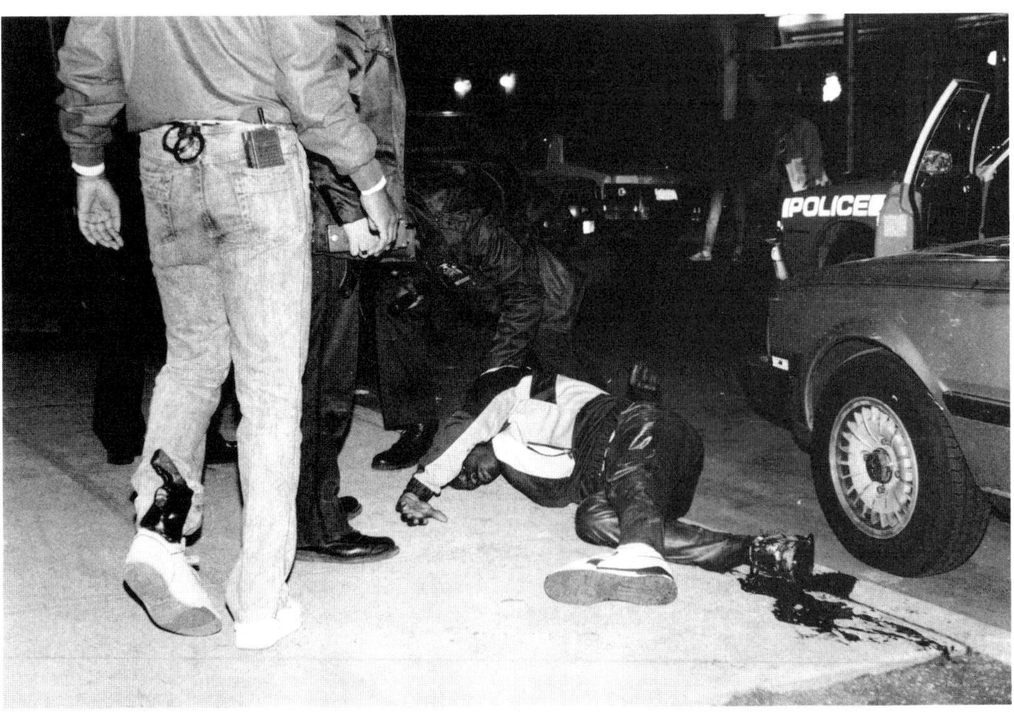

This young man, found with cocaine and crack in his car, shot himself while being pursued by police. The use of such drugs impairs judgment and can produce severe mood disturbances, greatly increasing a person's inclination to commit suicide.

Some suicidal teens may choose alcohol abuse as a way to kill themselves slowly.

Menninger believed that suicidal people had the wish to kill, the wish to be killed, and the wish to die. Some suicidal people, he said, chose alcohol or drugs as a way to kill themselves over a longer period of time. The suicide would take longer, but death eventually would be the result. The signs warning that someone is suicidal are similar to the signs for deciding whether a young person has a drug or alcohol problem. The young person often acts out at school and at home, has a change in eating and sleeping habits, and withdraws from friends and activities.

Among young people who have committed suicide, seven out of ten have used drugs frequently, half have had alcohol in their blood when they died, and three-quarters have suffered from drug or alcohol problems. There is no doubt among those who work with teens who have

attempted suicide that alcohol and drugs are major contributors to their attempts.

Parents who abuse drugs

Alcohol and drug abuse among parents also affects the teen suicide rate. Parental alcoholism frequently shows up in the background of suicidal young people, probably because family life is chaotic in homes where drugs and alcohol are abused. Substance abuse contributes to divorce, wife battering, incest, child abuse, and economic instability. All of these conditions also show up in the lives of suicidal young people. Many children carry feelings of hatred, revulsion, and anger toward their addicted parents. Sometimes they come to believe that the only way to escape their hostile feelings and their parents is through death.

Parents who abuse drugs and alcohol also set

an example for their children that drugs and alcohol are acceptable and that abuse of these substances can help people forget their problems. A seventeen-year-old high school senior in a support group for drug abusers was given marijuana by her mother. "There was always pot in the house," she told a reporter for the *Kansas City Star*. "My mom would smoke it and ask, 'Would you want some?' "

Some studies report that teen use of illegal drugs has dropped sharply in the past decade. In 1980, one-third of high school seniors said they had used marijuana in the past month. In 1990, only 14 percent said they had used it. Teens also report a higher disapproval of drug use. In some studies almost 90 percent of teens say it is wrong to smoke pot, and 95 percent disapprove of other drugs. Some think smoking and drinking has declined among the young, and that with a decline in drugs and alcohol, there will be a decline in suicides as well.

Suicidologists and therapists know that depression, drugs, and alcohol abuse play significant roles in the number of teen suicides. Depression and substance abuse also play large roles in the national suicide phenomenon known as "cluster suicides." In these suicides, drugs and alcohol help convince many young people in one school, city, or region that death is an acceptable solution to their problems.

5

Cluster Suicides

SUICIDOLOGISTS, SCHOOL counselors, and parents are particularly concerned about the growing national problem of cluster suicides. Cluster suicides occur when the suicide of one teenager sets off other teen suicides in a particular school, town, or area. These teens personally might have known the first teenager who committed suicide or they might have learned about the dead teen through the media.

Cluster suicides frighten and worry adults because it seems as if several teenagers suddenly have caught a suicide germ and no one knows where the germ will strike next. Suicide certainly is not contagious in the ways that diseases are. But therapists believe that among teens who are already inclined toward it, the suicide of a nearby teenager seems to spread the suggestion or desirability of the act.

(Opposite page) A woman mourns over the casket of her son, who was one of four teenagers involved in a suicide pact in Bergenfield, New Jersey. The rash of suicides in Bergenfield was the most widely publicized cluster of suicides ever.

Teenagers also seem susceptible to a type of cluster suicide known as copycat suicides. As in other cluster suicides, the suicide of one teen seems to encourage others to commit suicide. In copycat suicides, however, the suicide victims do not live in the same area and have no apparent connection to each other except the similarity of their deaths.

The first large-scale report of copycat or cluster

suicides came in 1774 when the German author Johann Wolfgang von Goethe wrote *The Sorrows of Young Werther*. In this romantic novel, Werther loves a young woman who is being pursued by someone else. Filled with sadness and jealousy, Werther shoots himself with his rival's gun.

Reports of suicide swept Europe after the novel was released, and many suicide victims were found with *Young Werther* next to their bodies. Wertheritis, as the suicide wave was known, prompted several countries to ban the book. Today cluster and copycat suicides often are referred to as the Werther effect.

Cluster suicides on the rise

Cluster suicides have become more common since the 1980s, but no one is sure why. They have been reported in Alaska, Arkansas, California, Colorado, Illinois, Indiana, Massachusetts, Minnesota, Missouri, Montana, Nebraska, New Jersey, New York, Ohio, Oklahoma, Texas, Utah, Virginia, Wisconsin, and Wyoming.

In Larimer County, Colorado, a dozen teens

Classmates express shock and disbelief after a young man shot himself during graduation exercises at a Massachusetts high school. Publicized suicides like this have resulted in cluster suicides across the country.

killed themselves during an eighteen-month period. In February 1986, three Omaha, Nebraska, teenagers killed themselves in five days, and others in the area attempted suicide. In Plano, Texas, between 1983 and 1986, nine teenagers committed suicide. In the 1980-81 school year, twenty teens took their lives in Fairfax County, Virginia.

A closer look at two separate instances of cluster suicides—four in Sheridan, Arkansas, and four in Bergenfield, New Jersey—show different ways in which cluster suicides can happen.

Cluster suicides in Arkansas

On March 28, 1990, Raymond Dale Wilkerson, seventeen, shot himself in his home in Sheridan. He left no note. A month later, Thomas Smith, also seventeen, a junior at Sheridan High School, stood up in front of his class, took out a concealed gun, announced his love for a girl in his class, and shot himself. That same night, Thomas M. Chidester, nineteen, a senior who knew Smith, wrote a note saying he could not go on any longer and shot himself in his grandmother's home. The next morning, Paul McCool, seventeen, a sophomore, shot himself in the head. He left no note.

The police and school authorities looked for a common thread among these four deaths—they could not find a link. The young men were not all friends, although they might have known of one another from school and around town. It appeared that each young man essentially was alone with his own problems and independently decided suicide was his way out.

News of the first Sheridan suicide traveled quickly in this town, and the second suicide intensified the local talk and newspaper, television, and radio coverage of the deaths. When the first young man died, news of his death made suicide seem like a more acceptable solution for the second troubled teen. With the second death, suicide seemed even more acceptable to the third, and even more so to the fourth teen.

Clusters in New Jersey

Police and school authorities could piece together much more information about the suicides that happened in 1987 in Bergenfield, New Jersey. The four teens in this most publicized of cluster suicides not only knew each other, they also chose to die together by gassing themselves in a car they left running in a closed garage. Many of the facts about their young lives are similar to the information experts have collected on the thousands of unhappy teens who attempt or commit suicide.

People who knew the teenagers described them as deeply troubled. Thomas Olton, eighteen, and Thomas Rizzo, nineteen, had dropped out of school. Olton had seen his father kill himself, and Rizzo had been treated for drug and alcohol abuse. Cheryl Burress, seventeen, also was a school dropout. Her sister Lisa, sixteen, had been suspended and talked about not going back to school. Their mother had remarried and the sisters were having a hard time adjusting to her new husband and his children.

When in school, all four were identified as members of the "burnouts," a group of angry, disgruntled kids who liked punk clothes and heavy metal music. All four were close friends with Joseph Major, the young man who had died a year earlier when he fell two hundred feet from the cliffs along the Hudson River. They brooded over his death, visited his grave, cried, and planned a death pact.

They filled Olton's 1977 Camaro with gas and parked it in an apartment complex garage. They took turns drinking alcohol and writing their

One of the four Bergenfield teenagers involved in a suicide pact is wheeled from the car in which the teens gassed themselves to death. They may have been influenced by the suicide of a close friend only a year before.

thoughts on a brown paper bag that became their suicide note.

Local people had mixed reactions to the young people's deaths. The police chief described them as kids who were "going nowhere fast." Some people in the area believed that had these hard-luck kids died separately, no one but their relatives would have paid much attention. But their decision to die together brought instant national publicity and drama to the story.

In the Chicago area

After the deaths of the New Jersey teens, Pamela Cantor, president of the National Committee of Youth Suicide Prevention, told *Newsweek* magazine: "We're going to have disturbed kids who are going to copy."

One day after the Bergenfield teens were found, two girls in Alsip, Illinois, a southside suburb of Chicago seven hundred miles from

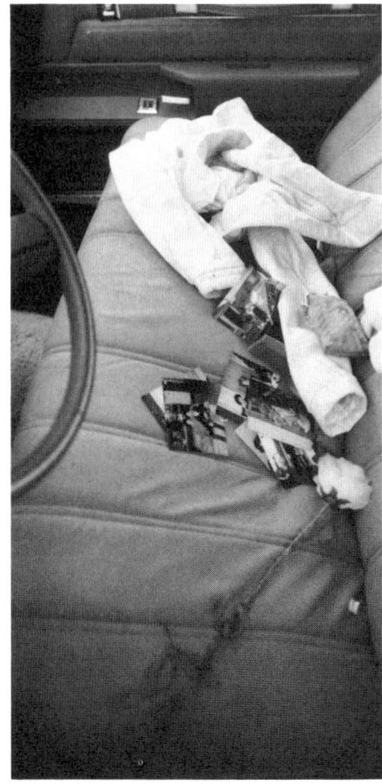

A rose and snapshots lie on the car seat where Nancy Grannan and Karen Logan were found after committing a copycat suicide.

New Jersey, died the same way. Nancy Grannan, nineteen, and Karen Logan, seventeen, probably had decided to kill themselves before the Bergenfield story broke, but the New Jersey teenagers showed the young women how they could die together. Grannan was sad over a failed marriage and two miscarriages. Both young women had dropped out of school, were recently unemployed, and were inseparable friends. They were found in Grannan's car with eleven suicide notes and Grannan's wedding album.

Elsewhere in Chicago a fourteen-year-old boy died in his car. News clippings about the Bergenfield and Alsip deaths were found in his room. Three days later in New Jersey a twenty-one-year-old woman and her seventeen-year-old boyfriend were found dazed from carbon monoxide in the same garage where the Bergenfield teens had died. Within the same week, other suicides by carbon monoxide poisoning were reported in New Jersey, Illinois, Nebraska, and Washington.

The media's role

These deaths, all occurring within a few days, rekindled an ongoing controversy about the role the media plays in cluster suicides. Does the news of one death encourage other teens to take their lives? Many experts have tried to answer that question. As with many things that are not clearly black and white, no one has a definite answer. Many people, however, have ideas about how movies and news coverage affect teens.

Several teens committed suicide after ABC-TV aired *Surviving* in 1985. Popular teen actress Molly Ringwald starred in this romantic drama of two teenagers who die in each other's arms from carbon monoxide poisoning. Two days after the movie was shown, a seventeen-year-old boy committed suicide with carbon monoxide. His father blamed his son's death on the television movie.

Authorities in Westchester County, New York, also thought cluster suicides in their area were related to *Surviving* and to the showing of *An Officer and a Gentleman*, a movie in which a young man hangs himself.

Movies and television

In 1981, the highly rated movie *The Deer Hunter* was said to have caused several suicides nationwide. The movie realistically showed the suicide of a troubled Vietnam veteran who dies of a self-inflicted gunshot wound to the head. Suicide numbers, particularly among young men, went up during the time the movie was being shown in movie theaters. Dr. Thomas Radecki, an Illinois psychologist, reported twenty-seven cases of gunshot wounds following viewings of the

A photographer stands at the entrance to the garage where the four Bergenfield teens committed suicide, and where a young couple later attempted suicide in the same manner.

A scene from the movie The Deer Hunter, *in which a troubled Vietnam veteran shoots himself to death. Some blamed the movie for the increase in suicides following the movie's release.*

movie, with twenty-four deaths resulting. On October 21, 1981, Radecki told a congressional committee, "I can comfortably estimate that 25 to 50 percent of the violence in our society is coming from the culture of violence being taught by our entertainment media."

Media effects studied

Dr. David Shaffer of Columbia University studied the suicide statistics following the appearance of four different television specials on teen suicide. Three of them, he found, were followed by an increase in suicides and suicide attempts. No excess suicides happened after the fourth special, which focused on the reactions of the surviving family members and included information about suicide hot lines.

Stories covering the suicides of famous people also seem to have a direct effect on the suicide numbers. California sociologist David Phillips discovered that in the month following the heavily publicized death of actress Marilyn Monroe, almost two hundred more people than would normally have killed themselves committed suicide.

He found that the suicide rate also was higher than normal following the death of comedian and television star Freddie Prinze. The star of the television comedy series "Chico and the Man" killed himself at the height of his popularity.

Several copycat suicides in Japan reinforced the belief of many professionals that publicity surrounding the suicides of famous people does bring more deaths. In 1986, Japan's top rock star, an idolized eighteen-year-old, jumped to her death from a seven-story building. The media reported Yukiko Okada was upset over a love affair that had gone wrong.

Two days after Okada's publicized death, two sisters, one eighteen, the other twelve, jumped to their deaths. A little more than two weeks later, thirty-three other teenagers had ended their lives. Another week later a twenty-one-year-old man jumped from the same spot where the rock star had jumped. Of the thirty-four suicides, twenty-two had jumped from buildings and one had in his pocket news clippings reporting the singer's suicide.

The suicide rate rose after Freddie Prinze (left), star of the popular television series "Chico and the Man," killed himself.

Media also can be helpful

Not everyone thinks the media is to blame for inspiring copycat deaths. In a 1987 *Newsweek* interview about cluster suicides, Charlotte Ross, executive director of the Youth Suicide National Center, said, "The media has gotten a bad rap." For every teen who commits a copycat suicide, she said, maybe a dozen others decide not to attempt suicide because of something they learned from a television program. One example occurred when the popular television show "The Facts of Life" handled the issue of suicide in one of its episodes. A young woman wrote to the cast and told them that watching the show had made her think twice about suicide as a solution to her problems.

Some suicidologists think dramas can prevent some suicides when they show how hard the suicide is on surviving family and friends. To be helpful, these dramas also must include some

information about suicidal warning signs and must provide national or area hot line numbers for suicidal people to call for help.

Media must be careful

In spite of the positive effects of some movies and television programs, the work and research studies of sociologist Phillips strongly indicate the media must be particularly careful when reporting suicides. Phillips found that the number of suicides climbed above normal following news stories in Los Angeles and Detroit newspapers about particular autocides that happened in those cities. Single-car auto fatalities increased by one-third in these cities during the three days following the news stories. The victims' ages were close to the ages of the victims described in the news reports. But in cities where newspaper strikes kept the public from reading about any suicides in the newspapers' publishing areas, Phillips found a drop in the expected suicide rate.

More research must be done before people will know with greater certainty what role movies, television, and newspapers play in suicide, and also what makes a teenager so susceptible to copycat suicides. Professor Madalyn Gould at Columbia University in New York says cluster suicides account for just 5 percent of teenage suicides. But, she says, people worry a great deal about these suicide epidemics because no one knows what sets off the suicidal behavior in groups of teens.

Some teens imitate others

Many therapists believe the idea of modeling helps to explain why some teens can become vulnerable to the idea of killing themselves when they hear about another's suicide. In modeling, people imitate others because they admire them or want to be more like them. Often, teens identify with another troubled person. They convince themselves they are having the same feelings or problems the suicidal person had.

People who knew the four Bergenfield teenagers, for example, said they had identified strongly with their outcast friend Joseph Major, who they believed had killed himself. When people called Major a loser, the four defended him and talked about how they were like him. The four friends' dress and actions fit some of the negative descriptions people applied to Major. The more others criticized the dead teen, the more the four friends believed they had to join him.

Teenagers, whether they are part of the "in" group or the "out" group, tend to imitate each other. They agree together what is good and bad in music and movies. They copy each other's fashions, hair styles, speech habits, and ideas. Sometimes these fashions and actions are copied from a popular singing or movie idol. Although a group of teenagers is made up of individuals, the people in the group try hard to look and act like each other.

Teens similar in cluster suicides

In a cluster suicide, the dead teenagers are similar to each other. They come from the same geographic area or school and from the same social or economic level. So, even if they do not know each other, they feel like they know each other, and they can identify with one another. If one teenager feels so miserable that he tries to kill himself, another teenager identifies with that suffering and begins to see suicide as a way to end his or her own pain.

Those who study suicide stress that not all teenagers are susceptible to copying the suicides

Teenagers tend to imitate the dress, hair styles, and actions of other members of the group to which they belong.

they hear about or see acted out in movies or on television. Millions of teenagers, for example, saw *Surviving* and *The Deer Hunter*, but only a handful killed themselves.

High-risk teens most vulnerable

Teenagers already at high risk for suicide are most likely to be affected by news of others' deaths. Coverage of these stories may in fact be the one thing that pushes an already suicidal teen over the edge into a cluster or copycat suicide. Researchers have interviewed young people who had attempted but did not complete their suicides. Those interviews have convinced many suicide experts that the news stories did not cause the suicide attempts, but that they probably reinforced the suicidal tendencies in a young person who was at high risk for suicide.

High-risk teens include young men who are

Students at Bergenfield High School react to the tragic news of their classmates' deaths. The teens involved in the suicide pact, like most suicidal teens, considered themselves outcasts and had school, family, and drug and alcohol problems.

known to have had a prior suicide attempt. "If a boy has tried once, there is enormous risk he will die of suicide within a year," says Dr. Gould. If the boy has a family history of suicide, he is twice as likely to commit suicide, she says, and if he is abusing drugs and alcohol, he is four times more likely to kill himself.

Risk factors among girls

Among girls, says Gould, the highest risk factors are depression, followed by substance abuse and a family history of suicide. Gould thinks it is useful to identify these high-risk factors for young men and women, but she knows there is more than one type of teenager at risk for suicide, even among those teens susceptible to cluster suicides.

When looking at the cluster suicides in Sheridan, Arkansas, Dr. Gould stressed the differences among the victims. Two of the four were members of the high school's Reserve Officers Training Corps. Only one had poor grades, and one might have had a drug problem. Two had relatives who had committed suicide, but none of the four was known to have made a prior attempt on his own life.

The Bergenfield teenagers, with their school, family, drug and alcohol problems, and feelings of being outcasts, shared more of the common characteristics associated with high-risk, suicidal teens. The two young women from Alsip, Illinois, who copied the New Jersey deaths, also had family, school, and work problems common among at-risk teens.

The diversity of these eight teenagers who died in cluster suicides reveals the difficulty facing parents, teachers, therapists, and school administrators when they try to identify which teens are at risk for suicide in general and cluster suicides in particular.

6

Prevention and Comfort

FOLLOWING THE DEATHS of the four teenagers in Bergenfield, New Jersey, more than three hundred parents and students filled the high school auditorium to blame school officials for the deaths. Why hadn't someone or something been there to help these young people? they asked.

School officials were quick to point out that the county had about thirty programs designed to help kids with their problems. The programs included Adopt-a-Cop for younger students and Project YES, which worked to build self-esteem in teenagers. At least six twenty-four-hour hot lines were available to anyone for crisis intervention. School administrators tried to remind the angry audience that even if there had been twenty more programs available, these new programs probably would not have touched or helped the Bergenfield teens. Some young people, they said, do not seek out this type of help.

Some students accused the school of not caring about its troubled kids. School officials, the students said, were too quick to push problem teens out. One young man told *Newsweek*, "I was a problem, so they asked me to leave. I felt worthless."

(Opposite page) Friends and schoolmates of Cheryl and Lisa Burress, two of the four Bergenfield teens who committed suicide together, console each other outside the funeral home. Following a suicide, people often feel such emotions as anger, defensiveness, grief, and confusion.

The school meeting helped to bring out the common emotions people feel after a teenager commits suicide: anger, defensiveness, grief, and confusion. These feelings were not unique to the people in Bergenfield. They are present in every school or community each time a young person commits suicide. These feelings often prompt school officials, parents, and other young people to work together to start a suicide prevention program in their school or community.

Schools develop programs

Many schools have developed programs specifically designed to reach young people before they come to believe that suicide is their only option. Some of these projects do not specifically deal with suicide but rather with helping young people feel better about themselves. Many educators believe that when young people feel positive about their lives in general, they will be less likely to focus on one or two problems that push them to suicide.

Drug education programs in schools may help young people say no to drugs, which are often a factor in teen suicides.

Aerobics, weight training, yoga, and diet education help students focus on fitness and health. Other courses on topics such as first-aid, rape prevention, family life, sex education, substance abuse, and self-esteem help teenagers gain more control over their lives. Talking about sex and drugs with a teacher and other students helps many teenagers avoid some of the problems that often drive young people to suicide.

In Muscogee County, Georgia, a school health program focuses on physical, mental, and social health for all ages. Students in kindergarten through sixth grade spend about two hours a week on health topics. Students in junior high and high school look at the social issues that affect young people.

Some schools have decided to tackle the issue

Many school curriculums include Shakespeare's play Romeo and Juliet, *in which two young lovers kill themselves. Using this play as a starting point, classroom discussion about suicide is encouraged.*

of suicide head on. For example, some curriculums include Shakespeare's play *Romeo and Juliet.* In this play, two teenagers from warring families fall in love. Rather than let their families' hatred separate them, they devise a plan to escape together. Mistakes and misunderstandings lead the young lovers to suicide.

Using this play as a starting point, teachers encourage students to talk about suicide. They write papers and hold class discussions on how Romeo and Juliet could have solved their problems in ways that did not harm them. They write new endings to the play and act out the revised scripts.

Peer counselors

Other schools have organized peer counseling groups. In these schools, young people are carefully trained in issues relating to schoolwork,

Academic pressures and the stress of leaving one's family and friends can be overwhelming for young college students.

family problems, drug and alcohol abuse, and pregnancy. These peer counselors are trained to listen to their schoolmates and to let adult counselors know when they think a young person is suicidal.

Some people have criticized peer counseling programs for putting too much responsibility and pressure on the teenagers who are trained to listen. Studies with teenagers clearly show, however, that nine out of ten of the young people who plan to commit suicide tell another young person about those plans. Whether adults like it or not, young people are more likely to know each other's death secrets, and because of this, they may be in the best position to help one another.

In Iowa's Nora Springs-Rock Falls Junior-Senior High School, the principal helped start a suicide prevention program that used the skills of young people. The school district agreed to devote a year-long course to suicide in the sophomore health program. The principal credited the resulting peer awareness of the suicide potential in other teens to directly saving students' lives.

College students vulnerable

In Chicago, a school recognized that young college students are particularly vulnerable to suicide because going away to college is stressful and removes the student from his or her old friends and support groups. To help its students make a smoother transition to college, the high school developed a course called "The Three Ds of College: Disillusionment, Doubt, and Depression." School officials hoped that talking about the stresses beforehand would help students cope with their first year away from home.

In Plano, Texas, the site of nine cluster suicides, the school and community established support groups for troubled teens. In Clear Lake

City, Texas, the site of other teen suicides, the school district hired specially trained psychologists to educate teachers and students about the warning signs for suicide. In New Jersey, more than three hundred educators were trained in suicide awareness.

Test for danger

Dr. Mary Jane Rotheram of Columbia University's Department of Child Psychiatry devised a simple test to help teachers determine if a student is in immediate danger of attempting suicide. Teachers, she said, should consider a teenager suicidal and should get the teen immediate counseling help if five of the nine factors are present:

- The student is male.
- There has been a past suicide attempt by a method other than swallowing pills.

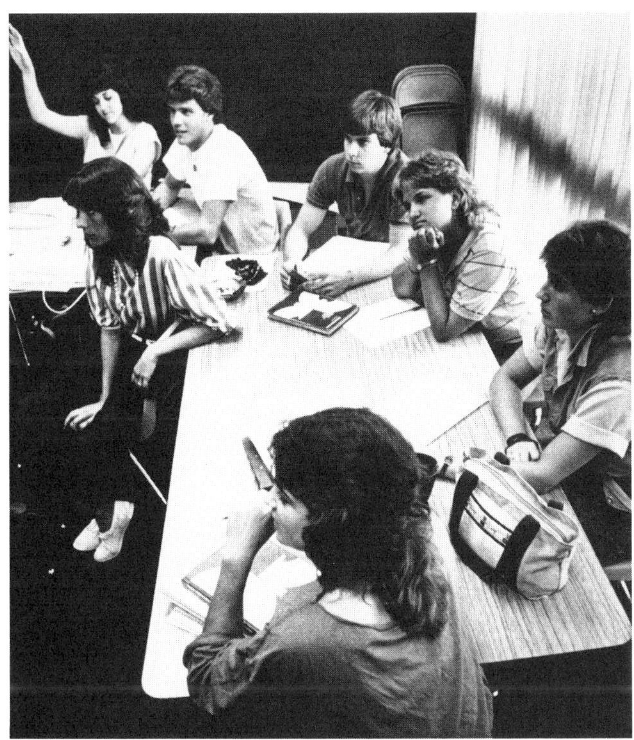

Following a rash of nine cluster suicides, high school students in Plano, Texas, participate in a class on dealing with adolescent stress.

- There has been more than one previous suicide attempt.
- The student has a history of antisocial behavior.
- The student has a close friend who committed suicide.
- The student has a family member who committed suicide.
- The student frequently uses drugs or alcohol.
- The student is depressed.
- There is friction between the student and the home or school.

In addition to trying to prevent suicide by training teachers and students in suicide prevention, many schools also have become sensitive to the need for postvention. Postvention focus is on caring for those who were close to or who knew the suicide victim and who feel confused and troubled by the death.

Postvention

Many schools call in professional suicide consultants after a student has committed suicide. These experts in youth suicide meet with groups of students and listen to their fears and feelings. They help the students talk through their thoughts about the death. Many students, for example, feel guilty. They worry that they should have been able to tell that their friend was suicidal. If they had an argument with their friend before he or she died or if they had not seen their friend for a while, they may worry that they did something to cause the suicide. Getting their feelings out in the open and discussing them with experts helps them see they were not responsible for the death.

Experts in youth suicide also help school officials walk the fine line between helping students express their grief and not appearing to be glorifying the death. Some people fear that suicidal teens may look at a large memorial service for a dead classmate and decide that they want to be remembered in this way as well. Officials in a Kansas school did not honor one mother's request that a page in the school yearbook be devoted to her son who took his life. She wanted him to be remembered by his classmates, but the school officials feared other teens might think, "If I kill myself, everyone will see my page in the yearbook."

The main objective of postvention is to keep other at-risk teenagers from attempting suicide. Schools must be sensitive to the possibility that other suicidal teens will become victims of cluster suicides, using one suicide as a reason to carry out their own suicidal ideas. The most sensitive time for at-risk students is within the weeks immediately following the suicide.

Young volunteers operate the phones at the Boston suicide prevention offices of the Samaritans, a group founded to help depressed and suicidal teens talk with other teens about their problems.

In spite of the widespread acceptance of suicide education and postvention programs, many schools strongly resist talking about suicide. They believe the all-too-common myth that talking about suicide will put ideas in young people's heads. The Rev. Michael Miller, a national speaker on teen suicide, recalled being swamped with students' questions after his suicide talk at a high school. The principal approached him later and said, "Boy, you caused a lot of problems." Miller replied, "No. The problems were already here. I just brought them to the surface."

Talking helps

Suicidologists and therapists strongly believe that talking about suicide is the healthiest thing anyone can do. Suicidal people already have been thinking about suicide. They will not get new ideas from someone else. Talking about those thoughts, the experts believe, helps reveal them to people such as teachers, school counselors, or

Most people believe that talking about suicide with teachers, counselors, friends, or others could help prevent many teenage suicides.

teenage friends who can then step forward to help the suicidal teen.

In 1991, Charlotte Ross, the director of the Youth Suicide National Center in San Mateo, California, said in an interview with *American Legion* magazine that she believed real progress had been made in preventing many teenage suicides. This progress, she believed, was being made in part through education in schools. "Kids now know that when they hurt and they're thinking of suicide, there are grownups around who won't think they're crazy and who will help without telling their parents or putting it on their school records, which we've found is what kids most fear."

An opposing view

Not everyone is pleased about the addition of suicide and death education to school curriculums. Samuel L. Blumenfeld, editor of the *Blumenfeld Education Letter*, believes death education in schools is responsible for the increased suicide rate among our nation's young people. Death education, he says, became acceptable in the 1970s as the medical and university communities tried to encourage people to be less afraid of dying and to see death as a natural part of life.

Blumenfeld believes there is a definite correlation between the introduction of classroom discussions on death in the 1970s and the rapid rise in teen suicides during the last twenty years. He believes classes on death and dying are desensitizing young people to the natural fear they should have of death and may be encouraging them to take their lives.

Death education teaches reality

Those who support death education believe that talking about the reality of death helps a young person understand that death is permanent and that young people's deaths leave a deep hole in the lives of those who knew and loved them. Many young people do not seem to understand that death is a permanent solution to a temporary problem.

Some young people who have survived their attempts have expressed ideas like this: "I didn't really want to die, I just wanted to be gone for a while to get away from my problems. I just wanted to be able to sleep for a long time and then wake up." Death education, educators say, helps teenagers understand that no one wakes up from death.

Author Francine Klagsbrun, who has written about teen suicide, said: "I do not believe that young people will be incited to suicidal behavior by hearing about it, but I do firmly believe that they will continue to be prevented from helping themselves and others by being falsely 'protected' from the subject."

Schools and communities have done a great deal to help young people prevent their own suicides or the suicides of their friends. The statistics, however, show that thousands of teenagers still die every year and their deaths have a sad and powerful impact on their friends and families.

Suicide survivors

In its suicide data sheet, the American Association of Suicidology (AAS) estimates that "Each suicide intimately affects at least six other people." The AAS report says, "Based on the number of suicides since 1970, it is estimated that the

A young woman who threatened to jump is lowered to safety by Boston police. Many young people who attempt suicide do not realize that it is a permanent solution to an often temporary problem.

number of survivors of suicides in the U.S. is 3.68 million."

What those numbers mean is that in a group of sixty-eight people, one person in that group has lost someone to suicide. The number of survivors grows by 180,000 people each year. "If there is a suicide every seventeen minutes, then there are six new survivors every seventeen minutes as well," says the AAS.

Suicide has been described as an act that not only takes the victim, but also takes a piece out of everyone who knew and loved the dead person. Professor Edwin Shneidman, who has devoted his life to the study of suicide, says he believes that "the person who commits suicide puts his psychological skeletons in the survivor's emotional closet." The victim, he says, sentences the survivors to an ongoing struggle with their own feelings of guilt. What could they have done to prevent the death? What, if anything, did they do to cause it? The "if onlys" torment the survivors. "It can be a heavy load," says Shneidman.

A friend of a Bergenfield teenager who committed suicide is comforted after learning of the tragedy. Suicide survivors can feel a wide range of emotions, including sadness, guilt, and embarrassment.

Survivors feel many emotions

The survivors feel a wide range of emotions. At first they feel shock, sadness, and a longing for the person to reappear. If the dead person had been a problem and had caused family and friends to worry, survivors may feel relief, but that relief only makes them feel guilty. Parents may worry that their other children will commit suicide, and they may focus on those children too deeply.

Some survivors believe the death was a sin and that the dead person will never reach heaven. For deeply religious people, the thought of a loved one spending eternity in hell gives them no peace. For many of them, their faith adds to the burden of their grief.

Students at Bergenfield High School express shock upon reading of the multiple suicides. Following the initial trauma of a suicide, survivors must pass through several stages in order to adjust to their loss.

Many parents of teenage suicides feel ashamed or embarrassed. They believe that others are looking at the family and saying to themselves, "Something must be wrong with them. Why else would their child have committed suicide?"

Outsiders do not know how to approach the family. Unlike deaths from illness or tragic accidents that prompt sympathy from outsiders, suicides make people uneasy, and many may stay away from the family at the very time when it needs support and comfort to work through its grief.

Help for survivors

Grief specialists encourage all survivors to express their feelings and to be patient while they go through the various stages of mourning. It is not unusual, they say, for people to spend two or more years working through their grief. Survivors must go through several stages as they pass from the pain of their loss to acceptance and, finally, to a fresh start.

First, they must accept that the death happened. Second, they must allow themselves to feel the pain of grief. Sometimes grieving people cannot eat. Some cannot sleep. Others get ill. People experienced in helping others cope with grief discourage the survivors from taking drugs to make them sleep or feel relaxed. Taking drugs will only slow down the grief process.

Adjusting to the loss

The survivors must learn to adjust to living and moving in the places where the dead person once was. Family members must learn to live in a home where their loved one is now missing. Classmates must adjust to not seeing their friend in school or on the football field or at play practice.

Finally, and most important, the survivors must reestablish and strengthen the relationships they have with others. Friends of the dead teenager must build new friendships. Family members must invest the love they had for their dead son or daughter, brother or sister, in the family members who are alive.

Writing about the loss of her fifteen-year-old stepsister who committed suicide, a girl named Bethany expressed the feelings of many survivors: "We miss you, Diana. We'll always miss you. You've left us with a tender ache that will never go away. But it's time to say good-bye to you and your dying. Your place is in our past. Our place is in the present."

Appendix

Facts About Suicide

Often people have misinformation about suicide. They remember the myths instead of the accurate information. Here are the facts people should remember about suicidal people:

1. People who talk about suicide probably will attempt or complete suicide.
2. Most suicidal people are ambivalent about dying and do not want to die.
3. Talking about suicide will not put the idea in someone's head. Talking about it helps reveal the person's feelings.
4. Suicide rarely happens without warning.
5. Someone is suicidal only for a short period of time.
6. Suicide is not inherited.
7. The majority of suicidal people are not mentally ill.
8. Suicide can occur in any ethnic, religious, racial, economic, or age group.
9. Most people who commit suicide have told someone their plans.
10. The danger of suicide is not over when someone starts to act and look better. In fact, most suicides happen within three months after the troubled person starts to feel better.

Suicide Warning Signs

If a teenager you know shows four or five of these warning signs, that young person probably is in danger of attempting suicide. Tell your parents, a teacher, a school counselor, or someone you trust about your friend so that he or she can get help. You could also call one of the hot lines listed in this book under "Organizations to Contact." If you must reach help quickly, dial 911. If your area does not have 911 service, dial 0 for operator. The operator will help you reach a crisis line.

Be concerned if your friend does several of the following:

- Talks about suicide or dying
- Gives possessions away
- Starts taking more risks
- Has trouble sleeping or suddenly sleeps too much
- Has trouble eating or suddenly eats too much
- Stops caring about his or her appearance
- Stops doing things with friends
- Starts to act out at school or at home
- Sounds self-critical
- Stops enjoying the things that once were fun

Signs of Depression

In the 1970s, Aaron T. Beck, a specialist in suicidal depression, with the help of his colleagues created the hopelessness scale. They found that the more people's answers matched the answer key, the more hopeless, and possibly suicidal, they felt.

Cover the answers with a piece of paper and answer each of the questions. How closely do your answers match the printed answers? If you have several similar answers, you might want to show this hopelessness scale to an adult you trust so you can talk about your feelings.

The Hopelessness Scale

Statement	*Answer*
1. I look forward to the future with hope and enthusiasm.	False
2. I might as well give up because I can't make things better for myself.	True

3.	When things are going badly, I am helped by knowing they can't stay that way forever.	False
4.	I can't imagine what my life would be like in 10 years.	True
5.	I have enough time to accomplish the things I most want to do.	False
6.	In the future, I expect to succeed in what concerns me most.	False
7.	My future seems dark to me.	True
8.	I expect to get more of the good things in life than the average person.	False
9.	I just don't get the breaks, and there's no reason to believe I will in the future.	True
10.	My past experiences have prepared me well for my future.	False
11.	All I can see ahead of me is unpleasantness rather than pleasantness.	True
12.	I don't expect to get what I really want.	True
13.	When I look ahead to the future, I expect I will be happier then I am now.	False
14.	Things just won't work out the way I want them to.	True
15.	I have great faith in the future.	False
16.	I never get what I want so it's foolish to want anything.	True
17.	It is very unlikely that I will get any real satisfaction in the future.	True
18.	The future seems vague and uncertain to me.	True
19.	I can look forward to more good times than bad times.	False
20.	There's no use in really trying to get something I want because I probably won't get it.	True

Source: M. Kovacs, A.T. Beck, and M.A. Weissman, "Hopelessness: An Indicator of Suicidal Risk," *Suicide*, vol. 5, no. 2 (Summer 1975), 98-103.

Glossary

alcoholism: Excessive dependence on alcohol, usually to the point where a person's body and mind are harmed.

ambivalence: Having conflicting feelings at the same time.

amphetamine: A drug that excites the nervous system.

anomie: Feeling detached or alienated from the world.

anorexia nervosa: A condition characterized by a complete loss of appetite with accompanying weight loss that may cause death.

autocide: Intending to commit suicide by causing a fatal car crash.

barbiturate: A drug that causes depression of the central nervous system, usually used to make a person feel less anxious or happier.

bulimia: An eating disorder in which a person periodically gorges with food and then induces vomiting.

cluster suicides: The occurrence of more than one suicide happening within a short period of time among people who live in the same area or attend the same school.

depression: A state in which the person feels hopeless, inadequate, exhausted, and unable to accomplish anything.

drug: Any substance that affects the body's functions when it is eaten, injected, inhaled, or absorbed into the skin.

drug abuse: The use of drugs for other than medical reasons.

egoistic: A view of the world that looks primarily at how things affect the individual.

heredity: Passing on traits from parent to child.

homicide: The deliberate killing of another person.

hot line: Phone number answered by people trained to help with problems.

manic-depression: Extreme mood swings from intense excitement and happiness to deep sadness.

marijuana: A plant whose leaves, stems, or flowers can cause feelings of euphoria when smoked or eaten.

modeling: Imitating or copying the dress, habits, styles, mannerisms, or attitudes of someone else.

parasuicide: A suicide attempt that has little chance of killing a person and that is used to draw attention to the suicidal person's wish to be helped.

PCP: The drug phencyclidine, which often is used illegally as a stimulant or a depressant.

postvention: Help given to friends and family after a suicide.

psychiatrist: A medical doctor who is trained to treat mental illnessess.

psychologist: A person, not a physician, trained to treat someone's emotional and behavioral problems.

psychosis: Abnormal behavior that includes losing touch with reality.

psychotherapy: Treating mental or emotional problems by using psychology.

schizophrenia: A severe mental illness in which a person withdraws and lives in a world of his or her own.

serotonin: A chemical in the brain that affects mood and behavior.

suicide: Voluntary, intentional taking of one's own life.

suicidology: The study of suicidal behavior and thinking.

Organizations to Contact

The following organizations deal with the issues of suicide. Some offer hot lines to help with crisis intervention and many offer publications and brochures on the topic.

The American Association of Suicidology
2459 South Ash
Denver, CO 80222
(303) 692-0985 (Monday-Friday, 9 A.M.-5 P.M. MST)

The association does not serve as a crisis line for people who feel suicidal, but it will give all troubled callers the phone number of their nearest crisis center. The association serves as a clearinghouse on information about suicide and offers pamphlets and information written for young people about suicide.

The American Legion
National Commission on Children & Youth
P.O. Box 1055
Indianapolis, IN 46208

This commission has a pamphlet called "Warning Signs: Suicide Prevention." It is written specifically to help young people recognize suicidal warning signs in their friends. The commission will mail a free copy upon request.

Covenant House
346 West 17th Street
New York, NY 10011-5002
(800) 999-9999

Covenant House works with homeless children who have run away from home or who have been abandoned. Many have fled abusive homes. These children frequently become victims of drugs, prostitution, and street violence. Because of their varied problems, many of these young people are suicidal. Covenant House has information on its services and on suicide. It works with suicidal teens, who can get referral help by calling Covenant House's 800 number.

Crisis Intervention and Suicide Prevention Center of San Mateo County
1811 Trousdale Drive
Burlingame, CA 94010
(415) 692-6662 (office)
(415) 692-6655 (crisis line)

This clearinghouse provides brochures and pamphlets to students and teachers about suicide. It consults with schools, counselors, and parents around the country but acts as a hands-on crisis center only for the people of San Mateo County. The center's staff, however, will mail information to anyone, regardless of where they live. Anyone can call its crisis line to get the phone numbers of the crisis centers nearest to them.

Father Flanagan's Boys Home
Boys Town, NE 68010
(800) 448-3000

This organization helps troubled teens and their families. The home's hot line can be called twenty-four hours a day, from anywhere in all fifty states and Canada. Its welcoming recorded message is in English and Spanish. The hot line's trained staff of counselors talked to more than 500,000 troubled and suicidal teens last year. The organization also provides information about Boys Town and its services.

National Center for Death Education
New England Institute
Mount Ida College
777 Dedham Street
Newton, MA 02159
(617) 969-7000, Ext. 249

The National Center for Death Education has library resources that deal exclusively with death, dying, and grief. Its library resources include books, pamphlets, articles, and 155 audio-visual tapes on death and grieving. Some of the center's materials specifically address suicide. The center also serves as a referral service to put people in touch with other agencies or resources dealing with suicide. During the summer the center sponsors summer workshops on death education.

The Samaritans
500 Commonwealth Avenue
Boston, MA 02215
(617) 247-0220 (24 hours)

The Samaritans provides information on suicide and the Samaritans program. The Samaritans services include talking to and befriending those who feel suicidal, depressed, or lonely. Suicidal teenagers living in Massachusetts and New Hampshire can call 1-800-252-TEEN for one-on-one comfort from another teen. Those calling from other states should call (617) 247-8050 between 3 P.M. and 9 P.M. EST, to talk to another teen about what is troubling them.

Suicide Hotline of Dade County

This twenty-four-hour hot line, located in southern Florida, helps suicidal people of all ages and counsels in Spanish and in English. Anyone calling from Broward, Dade, or Monroe counties should call (800) 560-6001. Anyone living outside those three counties should call (305) 358-HELP.

Almost every telephone book in the country lists phone numbers where suicidal people or their friends and family can get help. Look in the white or yellow pages under "Suicide" or "Suicide Prevention" for the names and phone numbers of agencies in your area that offer immediate help or referral services.

Suggestions for Further Reading

Anonymous, "I Wanted to Die," *Reader's Digest*, July 1987.

David L. Bender and Bruno Leone, eds., *Suicide: Opposing Viewpoints*. San Diego: Greenhaven Press, 1992.

David B. Bergman, *Kids on the Brink: Understanding the Teen Suicide Epidemic*. Washington, DC: PIA Press, 1990.

John Chiles, *Teenage Depression and Suicide*. New York: Chelsea House, 1986.

Warren Colman, *Understanding and Preventing Teen Suicide*. Chicago: Children's Press, 1990.

Richard Demak, "'And Then She Just Disappeared,'" *Sports Illustrated*, June 16, 1986.

Stanley L. Englebardt, "Teen Suicide: It Can Be Prevented," *Reader's Digest*, July 1987.

Dorothy Francis, *Suicide: A Preventable Tragedy*. New York: Dutton, 1989.

Margaret O. Hyde and Elizabeth Held Forsyth, *Suicide: The Hidden Epidemic*. New York: Franklin Watts, 1978.

Leslie McGuire, *Suicide*. Vero Beach, FL: The Rourke Corporation, 1990.

Michael Miller with Debra Whalley Kidney, *Dare to Live: A Guide to the Understanding and Prevention of Teenage Suicide and Depression*. Hillsboro, OR: Beyond Words Publishing, 1989.

Stella Pevsner, *How Could You Do It, Diana?* New York: Clarion, 1989.

Judie Smith, *Coping with Suicide: A Resource Book for Teenagers and Young Adults*. New York: Rosen, 1986.

Works Consulted

Associated Press, "Divorce Tops Death in Causing Depression," *Kansas City Star*, March 20, 1993.

Alan Bavley, "Teen-Agers Face Hostile World," *Kansas City Star*, October 25, 1992.

Samuel L. Blumenfeld, "The Teenage Suicide Holocaust: Is Death Education the Cause?" *The Blumenfeld Education Letter*, July 1990.

B. Bower, "Lethal Weapons: Gun Access and Suicide," *Science News*, August 15, 1992.

Barbara Barrett Hicks, *Youth Suicide: A Comprehensive Manual for Prevention and Intervention*. Bloomington, IN: National Educational Service, 1990.

Constance Holden, "A New Discipline Probes Suicide's Multiple Causes," *Science*, June 26, 1992.

Francine Klagsbrun, *Too Young to Die: Youth and Suicide*. New York: Houghton Mifflin, 1976.

Tamar Lewin, New York Times News Service, "Single Mothers Work, Worry and Do Their Best," *Kansas City Star*, November 9, 1992.

Larry Martz, "The Copycat Suicides," *Newsweek*, March 23, 1987.

Fran McGovern, "Children in the Abyss," *American Legion Magazine,* April 1991.

John L. McIntosh, "U.S.A. Suicide: 1990 Official Final Data," American Association of Suicidology, February 2, 1993.

Michael L. Peck, Norman L. Farberow, and Robert E. Litman, *Youth Suicide*. New York: Springer Publishing, 1985.

Howard Rosenthal, *Not with My Life I Don't: Preventing Your Suicide and That of Others*. Muncie, IN: Accelerated Development, 1988.

Jean Seligmann, "What Traditional Family? Debunking the Ozzie and Harriet Myth," *Newsweek*, December 7, 1992.

Edwin Shneidman, *Definition of Suicide*. New York: John Wiley, 1985.

"Teenage Suicide: The Ultimate Dropout," PBS Video, 1988.

Index

About the Author

Judith C. Galas has been a reporter and free-lance writer for fifteen years and has reported from Montana, New York City, and London. She has a master's degree in journalism from the University of Kansas and makes her home in Lawrence, Kansas.

Picture Credits

Cover photo by © Charles Gupton/Uniphoto

AP/Wide World Photos, 9, 14, 24, 33, 42, 54, 64, 84, 86, 89, 90, 91, 92, 93, 98, 105, 107, 110, 111, 112

The Bettmann Archive, 41, 52, 103

Donna Binder/Impact Visuals, 62

Gisella Cohen/Impact Visuals, 17

Kirk Condyles/Impact Visuals, 75, 80

Harvey Finkle/Impact Visuals, 45

Hazel Hankin/Impact Visuals, 56

Ansell Horn/Impact Visuals, 59

Evan Johnson/Impact Visuals, 102

Andrew Lichtenstein/Impact Visuals, 50, 63, 79, 81, 97, 104

Ken Martin/Impact Visuals, 70

Katherine McGlynn/Impact Visuals, 35, 49

Tom McKitterick/Impact Visuals, 61, 108

Stephanie Rausser/Impact Visuals, 30

Andrea Renault/Impact Visuals, 44

Reuters/Bettmann, 23

Linda Rosier/Impact Visuals, 65

Unicorn Stock Photos, 21, 27, 28, 29, 36, 72, 73

UPI/Bettmann, 6, 26, 32, 53, 58, 77, 100

Piet VanLier/Impact Visuals, 18

Jim West/Impact Visuals, 69

Steve Wewerka/Impact Visuals, 10, 66